To request permissions, contact tahmid@chowdhury.co.uk

If you ask nicely, I will probably say yes.

TAHMID
CHOWDHURY
— COACH & WRITER —

Contents

I.   Introduction

Diversity is about difference. It is what gives us such a rich set of different perspectives, views, and experiences.

We have seen a shift towards greater rights for women, ethnic minorities, disabled and LGBT+ individuals. There is also greater discussion around issues of class and religion from an equality perspective.

The discussion about diversity is often about increasing the participation of people from these groups. In the meritocratic, progressive societies that we aspire to live in, we want to ensure that we are making use of the skills and experiences of all people.

Unfortunately, this is not currently happening. Many individuals from minority or disadvantaged groups find themselves at a junior level where they are less included and have fewer opportunities in the workplace.

This experience can be hard to understand when as an individual we may not have experienced it for ourselves. For example, if we have found that the systems and institutions that we grew up with treated us well, how they might be tagged as not progressive or institutionally racist can be difficult to comprehend.

The idea of this book is to help you build your own understanding of diversity. This will help you understand yourself better and how your experience relates to, or might be different to other individuals.

I have found that senior leaders find the issues relating to diversity hard to grasp as they do not see it for themselves. At their level of the organisation, there are few diverse individuals who they interact with as peers. It is not something that they see in the same way individuals lower down the organisation might, where we can see greater levels of diversity entering the workforce depending on the sector.

Introduction

Some people also conclude that as there is growing visible diversity towards the bottom of an organisation that the issue of representation will fix itself. Over time, people will get promoted to more senior levels and representation will then happen.

But the real issues such as discrimination, disillusionment and despair are not visible to leaders. Managers further down the chain seldom report these issues upwards. It usually takes hard data and statistics to be able to shine any light on these issues in the first place. Getting such data is also an uphill battle.

It can also feel like a strange change-of-script when many leaders in organisations have risen the ranks by striving for excellence. They attended the most prestigious schools and universities, to now be told that such schools are elitist and not representative.

Senior leaders are far more prone to being criticised through their visibility and must deal with higher levels of scrutiny. From this perspective, it is understandable that the first reaction may be that this is another stick to be beaten with by shareholders, external stakeholders, or disgruntled staff.

This book looks to bring a new perspective to you as an individual. You may not have had that 'penny-drop' moment of understanding why we talk about diversity. I propose we do this by looking at our own background, highlighting experiences which influenced us growing up, compared to other individuals from different backgrounds and circumstances.

The aim of this is not to shame or suggest that you have done anything wrong throughout your life journey. Rather, it is to highlight how following a certain path has impacted you, and how someone else who took a different path may have had a very different set of opportunities and perspectives to you for that very reason.

I am very grateful for the time you are taking to read this book. I hope it will be a useful guide to understanding more about yourself and how you relate to others in the world.

Introduction

Why this book exists

This book sets out to help us better understand what we mean by 'Diversity.'

But this is not a book which will look to explain academic concepts in detail or put you through (another round of) unconscious bias training. This book will look to build your own understanding of what 'diversity' means to you.

For many of us, 2020 was a watershed year with the Black Lives Matter movement. The issue of race relations was brought front and centre. It left many people shocked and confused as to some of the fundamental premises they believed about the fairness of society.

This has led us to question some of the basic assumptions of our own upbringing and achievements. Many white professionals now find themselves questioning some of the underlying assumptions of their achievements, which can be painful and destabilising. Meanwhile, Black, Asian, and Minority Ethnic (BAME) individuals found the events traumatic for re-living past experiences or bringing hard-hitting realities back to the forefront of their minds.

Businesses have been particularly caught out by these events. When leaders tweet out support for Black Lives Matter, they find themselves criticised for being hypocritical as they are accused of not doing enough within their organisation to promote Black and BAME talent. This leaves leaders feeling particularly hamstrung and unclear as to what they should be doing. Staying silent is not the answer but speaking out can backfire. What should organisations be doing then?

This book looks to help you build your own understanding of the subject. I will not propose any cookie-cutter way that you 'should' think, rather I will introduce concepts and models to help you frame your understanding. This will give you far more confidence to engage with the subject. Throughout this book, I will also share my experiences to help give you a clearer understanding. After all, nothing quite gets a point across like a story.

The reason I am doing this is simple. In the push for greater equality, diversity and inclusion initiatives will only work if leaders genuinely believe in the importance of it. Many initiatives fail because they are seen as a tick-box exercise which is done for compliance rather than because leaders truly see it as important. So, by helping you understand the subject better, I hope that you will also care more, and take a greater active part.

Diversity and inclusion are predominantly driven by people who care about it deeply. In fact, you often see women, BAME, disabled and LGBT+ individuals working in these causes, but you rarely see those who are not part of these disadvantaged groups working in this space. If we have any hope of success, this pool needs to grow to include all of us.

This is not a step-by-step guide, as I do not believe such an approach works. Instead, I will arm you with a greater understanding of diversity and inclusion, using transformational coaching techniques which will help examine your thoughts on the subject in a safe, but thought-provoking way. I will also suggest further exercises to supplement your understanding.

My aim moreover is to build a greater understanding towards issues around diversity and inclusion. I hope in this way we can change the world to be a more caring, understanding, and inclusive society. Organisations have a key role to play in this shift.

I always love to hear from readers; you can connect with me on LinkedIn at https://www.linkedin.com/in/tahmidchowdhury1/ (you can scan the QR code below) or email me at tahmid@chowdhury.co.uk

Introduction

Who is this book for?

This book is aimed at people who are finding themselves needing further support in understanding diversity.

This book will talk from the perspective of corporate workplaces. I will reference leadership in particular, though leaders come in all shapes and sizes, up and down, inside, and outside of organisations.

If you are a manager, community leader, coach, or simply are just interested in understanding more about the book for yourself, you will also find this book very useful. I look to keep awkward and unintelligible corporate speak to as little as possible so that anyone can make the most out of this book.

I also wrote this book to support practitioners working in the space of diversity who are looking for additional supporting material when working with senior leaders. Having worked in this space myself, I understand how difficult it can be to get backing to discuss the subject (let alone approval for initiatives!).

Many of us are passionate about diversity in all its forms. However, we were not born this way, instead, we were prompted to care about it due to something we saw or experienced. I believe it is our role to help others go on a similar journey.

Wherever you are on your own understanding of the subject, this book will support you in understanding what diversity means to you. I hope that it will bring down the walls of this being a 'no-go' area, and one that you are far more comfortable engaging in. From there, you will have the opportunity to make impactful change.

I.   Understanding diversity

To address diversity issues, first, we must understand what we mean by it.

This chapter will look to introduce you to the general concepts used when we refer to diversity. We will set out why diversity is being talked about and what we mean when we talk about diversity.

We will also look at some of the terminology to become more familiar with the subject.

By understanding diversity better we will be able to continue our path to our own understanding later in the book.

I will give my own understanding of diversity for your benefit. I have looked to keep the concepts and terminology as easy to read and understand as possible. They are generally short-and-sweet explanations based upon working assumptions, rather than denser academic definitions.

This will allow you to get a good level of knowledge without needing to dive into additional resources, though you may decide to do so later down the line.

What we mean by diversity

Diversity is about difference. There are all sorts of diversity – biodiversity, cultural diversity, diversity of thought, place, subject, interests and so on.

Here, we refer to diversity from the point of view of people. In other words, embracing the differences between people to bring a greater whole. For many organisations, the goal is to have a workforce that represents the population.

In a world where more individuals are coming from ethnic minority backgrounds, do not define as cisgender (where someone's gender is the same as the one they were born with), 'straight', and have disabilities, we are seeing a wider range of individuals coming into the workplace. This is on top of cultural shifts such as an increasing number of women who work compared to only a generation or two ago.

From a workplace perspective in the UK, we often look at the characteristics listed within the Equality Act 2010[1]:

- Age
- Disability
- Gender Reassignment
- Marriage and civil partnership
- Pregnancy and maternity
- Race
- Religion or belief
- Sex
- Sexual Orientation

The Equality Act sets out that it is illegal for individuals to be discriminated against, either directly or indirectly, based on the above characteristics.

---

[1] https://www.gov.uk/guidance/equality-act-2010-guidance

As this is a legal requirement, all organisations are obligated to comply with these areas as part of the law. It is why jobs cannot be advertised for men or single individuals only, for example.

Other countries have similar laws with different definitions, but the fundamental underpinning tends to be the idea of non-discrimination.

Whilst the Equality Act gives legal status to this area, I see it as a minimum-level standard. Rather than looking to include, it is essentially telling firms not to discriminate. It is compliance-based in nature, and therefore does not address some of the cultural issues faced in the workplace or in society.

Diversity efforts within business a few decades ago have focussed on bringing more women into the workplace. We have seen growing efforts to improve representation throughout the talent pipelines, Science, Technology, Engineering and Mathematics (STEM) subjects up to senior level.

While doing this, barriers have become evident – for example outdated maternity leave practices that penalise women for having children by not considering them for promotion. Firms have had to go much further than the Equality Act.

Whilst these efforts have been broadly successful in bringing in women to firms, there is usually a point within organisations where progression becomes more difficult towards the middle to higher end of the organisation. This is what is often referred to as the 'glass-ceiling', where women are often not able to break through due to a lack of opportunities, mentorship, or access to senior leadership which prevents them from getting the necessary exposure to go further.

This is also on top of any other cultural issues relating to wider expectations. For example, women are often the parent that is the primary caregiver for children or elderly relatives. Women can feel intimidated being 'the only one' in industries with little gender diversity, which adds to the feeling of adversity and lack of support.

Race

More recently, race has become particularly prominent, notably so following the events of Black Lives Matter. BAME employees are increasingly entering the workforce. However they can enter lower-level entry jobs, and in many fields often do not make it past middle-management. BAME individuals face certain similar challenges as women in terms of not being included. (Unless of course, you are a BAME woman in which case you will have challenges on both sides).

I once heard that the solution in an organisation for getting more women into an organisation was to 'hire more daughters and sisters' of the men already within the organisation. This worked to an extent with the growing number of educated women coming into the workforce. However, for BAME individuals this does not work. Nor is it an ideal situation when talking about opening access to an organisation more widely.

Organisations are now realising there is a need to widen the net. Therefore, we have more efforts to hold open evenings, a wider range of university campus recruitment events as well as outreach talks. Without going to where BAME people live, it is unlikely that an organisation is going to attract a wider range of BAME talent to apply for its organisation.

LGBT+

Representation of LGBT+ tends to be relatively stable up to senior levels, though this is generally white, gay men as opposed to other parts of the LGBT+ group. Nevertheless, the ability for someone to 'come out' in the workplace (and society) can widely vary. This has effects on wellbeing as well as mental health. It should also be mentioned that the 'T' – i.e., transgender have particularly high levels of discrimination and issues around the workplace.

For example, gender reassignment can cause HR complications due to systems not being built for the needs of transgender individuals, which often leads to a lot of pain and effort, not to mention issues relating to whether colleagues will be open and supportive of them. More basic issues include being able to complete online forms where there are only options for male or female, which unintentionally negatively effects staff who do not identify with a specific gender.

Other Areas

Disability is an area that is likely to become more prominent over the next decade, and efforts are already being made to increase workplace accessibility. However, representation rates still are very low at senior levels, with a strong assumption of 'ableism' to become a leader. Although we often think of disability as something visible, many disabilities can be invisible.

Additionally, age discrimination is an area of focus which may often go under the radar, as many organisations are becoming younger in demographic; older staff are sometimes getting pushed out of their organisation and undervalued for the experience they bring to their roles.

Religion, marital status, and pregnancy tend to be dealt with in a more compliance mindset within organisations. These are additional areas where more can likely be done but often are implicitly handled elsewhere – particularly pregnancy which tends to be covered in wider gender issues for women. Religion does tend to get some focus. Some organisations do make efforts to celebrate a wider range of religious events, as well as having areas such as prayer rooms for those practising.

Similarly, marital status is not an area where much research has looked at whether discrimination takes place – particularly in organisations. From what I have heard anecdotally, it can work both ways in that married individuals with children can be allowed to go home earlier because they need to, leaving younger individuals without families more work and longer hours.

Alternatively, I do not doubt that implicit bias can take place during recruitment, particularly of married women who might be expected to go on maternity leave. This leads to issues such as women taking off their wedding rings during an interview as companies are known for not wanting to hire women who may be due to have a child within the next few years.

13

Areas not covered in the Equality Act

A regular comment is what is *not* included under the Equality Act. There is no focus on class or socio-economic background. This is an area where growing interest lies, as it becomes apparent the economic division of the North and South of England, as well as other disparities across the UK. There is a growing will to do more to ensure opportunities are more evenly distributed to those from deprived backgrounds. These individuals may not be protected or supported otherwise, e.g., if they are white working class.

To date, no legal duty has been placed upon protecting those from lower socio-economic backgrounds. Nonetheless, organisations have looked to incorporate some elements of this in their diversity programmes, and there is a growing movement to improve social mobility within society, such as through the Social Mobility Foundation.

From my perspective, whilst this is welcome, we often lack the data to truly know whether someone has come from a lower socio-economic background or not. Certain organisations may be doing well on this, but we do not necessarily know as it is not visible. Those who have come from lower socio-economic backgrounds have talked about how they had to change their accents to fit in.

I believe that the Equality Act is a helpful start to consider diversity, even if it could go further and be enforced better. But it also does not stop anyone from doing more either, whether it be socio-economic background or something else. We could do more to include different accents or regional voices, nationalities, or political views if we want to.

There are also a few other provisions in the Equality Act that are worth knowing. For Public Bodies, there is the Public Sector Equality Duty.[2] This obliges Public

---

[2] https://www.equalityhumanrights.com/en/advice-and-guidance/public-sector-equality-

Bodies to ensure that all individuals are considered when developing policies and carrying out day-to-day work. It also means that Public Bodies must have due regard (but not necessarily tackle) the need to:

- Eliminate Discrimination
- Advance equality of opportunity
- Foster good relations between different people when carrying out their activities.

The Equality Act also gives provisions for Positive Action. This is **not** Positive Discrimination, which is illegal. Positive Action in recruitment allows employers further flexibility in meeting their goals for greater representation.

For example, if an organisation had two applicants for a job who had both passed the interview and were deemed fit for the role, the Positive Action Provision would allow them to hire a BAME or disabled individual over the other person if they wished to make use of the provision. The idea behind this is to allow greater flexibility within recruitment to promote diverse talent. It is not without an element of controversy, but this is often mischaracterised as hiring for diversity's sake.

Any individual being hired would have needed to pass the necessary benchmark and interview to benefit from the provision, so we are not talking about going into the street and hiring whoever to hit a representation target - they would need to be qualified for the job.

duty

Why we talk about 'diversity'

'Diversity', 'Diversity and Inclusion', and sometimes 'Equity, Diversity and Inclusion' is a complex and growing area.

Focus on diversity from a business-perspective is taking a more critical look at how our organisations are made up, and the people who work in them. This has become a growing area of interest as our societies have become more diverse. For example, here are some statistics from the UK:

- As of 2011, 14% of the UK are ethnic minorities. This number will increase with the next census in 2021. Over 40% of people in London are ethnic minorities.[34]
- 1 in 2 young people (18-25) did not define as "100% straight" in a YouGov poll from 2015[5]
- 19% of Working Age Population reported they have a disability[6]

Our society is becoming increasingly diverse. We are not talking about one or two diversity hires either, we are now talking about a sizeable number of customers and employees that will fall under at least one protected characteristic. This is without looking at women at senior levels which is still lagging behind, despite making up half of the population. Nor does it examine the more nuanced questions of social mobility or class. This also excludes many other ways this can be examined, such as diversity of thought or experience more broadly.

---

[3]https://www.ons.gov.uk/peoplepopulationandcommunity/culturalidentity/ethnicity/articl es/2011censusanalysisethnicityandreligionofthenonukbornpopulationinenglandandwales/ 2015-06-18#:~:text=4.-
,Ethnicity%20of%20the%20non%2DUK%20born%20population,African%2FCaribbean %2FBlack%20British

[4] https://www.nomisweb.co.uk/census/2011/QS201EW/view/2013265927?cols=measures

[5] https://yougov.co.uk/topics/lifestyle/articles-reports/2015/08/16/half-young-not-heterosexual

[6] https://commonslibrary.parliament.uk/research-briefings/cbp-7540/

Understanding diversity

Diversity is not a fad or a phenomenon that will die out any time soon. As younger generations from ever increasingly different backgrounds enter adulthood, it is important that we learn to value them as employees and customers alike.

The urge for more action relating to diversity and inclusion is growing every day. As has been illustrated by the events of 2020, this is no longer one that can be ignored. Furthermore, the recent cost of living crisis being felt across the world has been difficult, and it has affected those from disadvantaged communities in particular.

If businesses and organisations expect to serve an increasingly diverse set of customers or attract and retain the best talent within an increasingly diverse workforce, we must make diversity a fundamental part of how we form our actions and activities.

There is a growing amount of literature which demonstrates that a more diverse organisation performs better financially. The influential report, 'Why Diversity Matters' by McKinsey highlights that:

- Companies in the top quartile for racial and ethnic diversity are 35 per cent more likely to have financial returns above their respective national industry medians.

- Companies in the top quartile for gender diversity are 15 per cent more likely to have financial returns above their respective national industry medians[7]

If you would like to understand more about the business case for Diversity, I would highly recommend reading the McKinsey report, as well as its subsequent reports 'Delivering through Diversity' and 'Diversity Wins: How inclusion matters' available online.[89]

---

[7] https://www.mckinsey.com/business-functions/organization/our-insights/why-diversity-matters

[8] https://www.mckinsey.com/business-functions/organization/our-insights/delivering-

Understanding diversity

The conversation about diversity is also being driven by societal conversations. Aside from Black Lives Matter, there are often conversations around issues such as LGBT+ rights in different countries, rights on abortion or other political issues.

Businesses are increasingly expected to take a view on social issues, meaning that it is harder to simply ignore these issues. We should also not forget that businesses are made up of people, many of which will come from these different groups. It is a matter of employee wellbeing and integrity for a business to have a consistent view of what they say internally and how they respond externally.

I recall speaking to a former colleague of mine at my former department within the UK Government. They expressed their rather obvious disappointment about how the department had talked about how much they believed in diversity and inclusion yet brought staff together to announce that the department was pulling out of Stonewall, the pioneer LGBT+ organisation. Supposedly Stonewall had been too political, which therefore meant the department could not be associated with it any longer.

It does not take a historian to realise that the Stonewall Riots was a political movement in its nature. It was fighting for the gay rights movement. This act left a bitter taste for staff who had heard so much being espoused about the importance of diversity within the organisation.

The negative experience was also much greater for LGBT+ employees who now saw their employer actively disassociating with Stonewall. Many of these staff ended up leaving.

---

through-diversity

[9] https://www.mckinsey.com/featured-insights/diversity-and-inclusion/diversity-wins-how-inclusion-matters

Why diversity matters to me

When people first told me about the idea of diversity and inclusion, I honestly glazed my eyes. I questioned the premise of it. I was a fresh university graduate entering the world of work. I was completing a few different internships and was just learning what a 'good' corporate environment looks like.

I assumed that the workplace was an open, tolerant, and meritocratic space. So the idea of diversity amounted to tokenism. In hindsight, this was rather naïve. As my starting point was believing that office-spaces would be doing what I now brand 'inclusive practices', I did not understand the point of why this push for corporate diversity mattered.

I understood that there was a lack of representation at the top, but I simply assumed this to be a generational thing – somewhat selfishly I assumed that the previous generation did not have the same educational background as me, therefore they did not get to rise to the top.

Unlike them, I was a university graduate with a host of extracurricular activities and a keen will to succeed – everything I had been told to do to be successful. I presumed that hard work and excellence would push me to the top, and I was willing to do the hard yards without needing to use the badge of being a diversity hire.

My conceptions quickly came crashing down though once I learnt more about corporate culture. I once joined a very poor working environment, where people would not speak in the open, instead messaging each other on the internet in case they got overheard. After a phone call, I heard my head of team who got called by someone, put down the phone and say "f***head".

Worse still, once again I naively believed the positive ideals of 'bring your ideas' and a 'fresh pair of eyes' were universal factors across organisational workplaces. This quickly made me fall foul of the system, and I was quickly branded a troublemaker. This led to performance ratings of being 'negative' and incompetent within my job. Unfortunately, once I fell into this hole, it was incredibly difficult for me to rebuild my reputation. It was not long before I was carted out the door.

Happily, I have since rebuilt my career and have been successful thus far. Nonetheless, I will never forget how harrowing the experience was, and how much a workplace can quickly turn against people when it is not open to honest views and opinions. I later learnt that as an individual coming from a South Asian background, these stories happen fairly frequently. Whilst this behaviour may sound shocking to you, it generally is not for individuals working in the diversity space.

I have often spoken to older BAME colleagues who have scars on their backs from similar experiences –tales describing managers with a vendetta, borderline illegal workplace practices and quite blatant discrimination. Those that have survived in the workplace following such experiences, they are often wary of being exposed in such a way again. It is no wonder why so many of them look to keep their heads down when such topics come up. If you wonder why there are BAME people not saying anything, this is probably why!

What is interesting is that I also can have conversations with other colleagues, often white, who cannot relate to this experience at all. It is particularly stark when it is based within the same organisation and even the same team. I recall telling my own stories to my colleagues and them being genuinely shocked at how I had been treated. At first, it was a question of perhaps having bad luck with a manager or team, however, when examining the patterns of behaviour that people like me experienced, it became evident that there was an underlying trend.

For me, working on diversity means addressing these underlying issues that happen daily – staff from pretty much every underrepresented group – BAME, women, LGBT+, disabled, religion, older staff etc. tend to have a worse experience. This is often reflected through higher rates of discrimination, bullying and harassment, and lower levels of happiness. This means a greater likelihood to be passed over for a promotion and far more likely to receive lower performance markings and bonuses.

I am no longer surprised by the negative statistics that come out of surveys relating to diversity. I have heard such stories often enough that the more shocking thing is how little people talk about them.

Understanding diversity

Many issues are swept under the carpet – be it the open secret of the high-performing boss who treats people terribly, the mysterious story of someone being carted out the backdoor over the weekend with no one being told why, or a blind eye on strange management practices deemed too difficult to address. Whilst everyone suffers from these issues, those from minority backgrounds tend to suffer more.

I also hasten to add that diversity is not all about problems. In its nature, we are talking about bringing differences together, and valuing the experience of different individuals. I have learnt so much by working in this space about issues I would never have heard of otherwise.

I have greatly enjoyed learning from colleagues speaking passionately about causes they care about, the most prominent examples for me have been Holocaust Memorial Day and Black History Month.

Let us not forget that having a diverse, inclusive team builds excellent strengths. A group with no women is likely to pass over many key observations about how a product may not be practical for females (e.g., because it does not consider different sizing), and individuals who are from an ethnic group such as a Sikh background may be better able to actively engage local communities around an event to increase participation.

I have been greatly humbled by the predecessors that have worked in this space before me, many of which have done so for decades at a time when few of us had even heard of the term 'diversity' from a corporate perspective. So, whilst the statistics often look quite bad, they would have been even worse if it were not for the pioneers championing this cause over the last few decades. This has come at the cost of their careers and their wellbeing.

I am driven to work on this agenda because I care about diversity. I believe it is vital for us to build a better and more inclusive society which truly values people over processes.

Why we speak about diversity as a collective

As you may have noticed, I have used the word diversity to cover a whole range of different characteristics and identities. Diversity covers a lot of things.

A fair criticism of using the word diversity is that it tends to generalise and impersonalise the issues which are felt by individuals. If we were to look at this more closely, the issues that women face would be different to what a BAME individual might face, and the issues for a disabled individual could also be very different as well. By lumping these groups together, we risk conglomerating all problems into one.

So, if there are issues discussing diversity so broadly, why do we continue to do so?

We have seen many different movements and groups, both in society and in the workplace. Race activists fought for racial equality, and women activists fought for gender equality. These topics were seen as quite separate.

It becomes evident that by bringing together this diverse group of underrepresented individuals, there is a level of commonality between all of them. Each group would benefit from equal rights and the ability to succeed in society. So everyone would benefit from more inclusive and supportive environments.

As such, we have seen a trend of these different groups coming together to better advocate for broader rights. By taking a common stance, the voice for diversity is amplified.

Different groups have already done this for themselves. We take for granted that gay and lesbian rights are the same issue, however historically in the USA, these were first campaigned upon separately. It was only by realising that bringing together these groups would they be able to unite their voices. Then came bringing further awareness around bisexuality, and we are now seeing a greater understanding of transgender, queer, intersex, asexual and other identities. Indeed, we are still seeing friction around those saying that transgender rights should not be a part of the LGB group, and these voices include those who are lesbian, gay, or bisexual. So clearly such groupings are not to be taken for granted.

Similarly, neurodiversity is now being used as a term to capture the different ways people's brains work. This can include people with ADHD, autism, or another 'condition'. As we will explore, BAME is a contested term, but ultimately comes from a desire to highlight the collective experience of underrepresented groups which often face additional levels of discrimination.

So, there is certainly a benefit in bringing together groups of people. My way of framing this is about tackling different levels of an issue. For example, sometimes we are talking about a specific individual group such as the issues faced by black, married women in the workplace. These will be different to those who are just 'black', 'married' or 'women'. This group may have issues with their abilities to progress within their workplace. However, this is also a relatively small sample size, and it may be easier to hypothesise or get data from a bigger group, such as ethnic minority women more broadly.

Naturally, the experience of Asian women may be different from a black woman, but by looking at the different trends we have a better idea of what may be happening. We can also take a larger grouping to be able to better encapsulate a broader narrative, such as looking at women in the workplace. This can then become a wider inclusivity issue, meaning a diversity strategy which looks at including and empowering different voices can help tackle the issue at a macro level.

I do strongly advocate that we take a granular approach as well. A diversity and inclusion strategy is not about a one-size-fits-all approach to any underrepresented group. Some issues need a more targeted approach, for example having accessible software for disabled staff or flexible working for carers or parents.

Nonetheless, the principles behind creating a more compassionate and supportive environment are critical. Creating such an environment is far more powerful than having an individual race, gender and disability strategy which will likely be too narrow and targeted to have any real impact in isolation.

How we use terminology

Some of the terms that I use may be different to what you have previously seen. For example, in the UK we have tended to use BAME to signal Black, Asian, and Minority Ethnic, however many individuals do not like using it. Some organisations are starting to move away from such wording. In the US, the term tends to be 'People of Color', which is a little odd to me in the UK as using the term 'coloured' is deemed offensive. I recognise that these may be ones that you are less familiar with or even terms with which you disagree. I do not aim to be the arbiter of right or wrong.

Likewise, the idea that LGBT+ rights were one unified force was not always the case. It's also worth noting that I use LGBT+ as the term I am most familiar with, but this has also shifted and some use longer acronyms including Queer, Intersex Asexual. The terminology is continuously evolving.

It can be easy to get overwhelmed by the number of different terms. Whilst it is important to keep on learning, the best solution is often just to ask in a curious and open-minded way. People in these groups are used to people not knowing what a term means, so if you ask politely and respectfully, they are usually happy to explain the idea to you. This is best done to someone you know directly and doing so privately. This is as opposed to asking people who post on social media about these issues. This can put them under pressure to educate people, often in quite a combative discussion.

I also note that there are words that are now deemed offensive which were commonly used several decades ago. If in doubt about the appropriateness of using a word, you may ask someone trusted. Failing that, you may also search the internet with something along the lines of 'is saying xxx appropriate'.

Grouped terminology such as BAME and LGBT+ help us as a shorthand to list each one individually. This helps with data collection, which is so key to better understand the experiences of these groups.

Nonetheless, it is important to remember that looking only at BAME can be problematic. For example, the Black Lives Matter movement has highlighted that there are problems relating to Black Americans. Whilst other minority groups also face issues, it is likely to be felt differently or less severely. The UK Government website, Ethnicity Facts and Figures highlights these disparities quite starkly. For example, taking the data of Stops and Search, this happens to 4 White individuals per 1000. For Black individuals, this is 38 per 1000. Interestingly, Asian is 11 per 1000. As we can see, there is a particularly high rate for Black individuals. Whilst the Asian statistic is higher than White individuals, it is still far less of an issue.[10]

To take my own perspective, I can also be referred to as Asian. I sometimes refer to myself as South Asian to make it clearer what part of Asia I am referring to. This is also different to the US where 'Asian' can often refer to what we would refer to as East Asian in the UK, for example, those of Chinese descent.

However, I am an Asian of Bangladeshi background; the stats show that the Stop and Search rate for Bangladeshis are 21 per 1000, which is statistically high; the Asian statistic is averaged down predominantly by Indian ethnicity individuals, where the rate is 4 per 1000, the same as White individuals.

Indian migrants historically tended to be from middle-class backgrounds with higher education levels, compared to Bangladeshi who tended to be from working-class backgrounds. This plays out across the stats, where we see Bangladeshis having lower incomes across the board, and it is a lesser-known fact that most 'Indian' restaurants are run by Bangladeshis. What this means in practice is that someone who looks like they are from a similar group may have very different life experiences.

For example, from 2018 data, on average Bangladeshis and Pakistani ethnicities earned £9.62 per hour, compared to Indian ethnicities earned £13.46 per hour. Interestingly Indian Ethnicity earnings are higher than White British, who earn £11.90 per hour.[11] So the general earnings of Bangladeshi and Pakistani

---

[10] https://www.ethnicity-facts-figures.service.gov.uk/crime-justice-and-the-law/policing/stop-and-search/latest

[11] https://www.ethnicity-facts-figures.service.gov.uk/work-pay-and-benefits/pay-and-income/average-hourly-pay/latest

ethnicities are significantly lower than Indian ethnicities, despite looking similar on the street.

These are averages, so my own experience as a relatively well-off Bangladeshi may be more anomalous than the norm. I grew up in Bath, which was relatively posh and received a fee-paying school upbringing. Many other Bangladeshis live in East London, where there is a higher level of poverty, and Stop and Search is more likely to be in place.

My own experience illustrates how complex this subject can be; the deeper we go the more additional complexities we find. This is not just for race, but also other groups such as LGBT+, where we tend to see visible LGBT+ being represented at senior levels by gay men. We see far fewer 'out' lesbian women.

So, these grouped terminologies help us understand the bigger picture of what is happening. But we are still people, and individual life experiences will greatly vary from what is considered the norm.

Intersectionality

A growing concept is an idea of 'intersectionality'. Intersectionality is the idea that people cannot just be put in one box and may be a part of several different groups.

For example, we have previously discussed race and LGBT separately. What if that LGBT individual was also BAME? What if they are also a woman, and perhaps also disabled?

A more intersectional approach has been taken where it has become evident that taking one characteristic does not fully cover the issue. For example, whilst we have seen an increase of women in the workplace and at senior levels, these have predominantly been white women. BAME women have been left behind.

Some organisations are now looking to therefore focus specifically on BAME women. There is growing recognition that what has been done to promote women in the workplace has not taken their needs into account.

In general, being from two minority groups tends to increase negative experiences in the workplace. BAME individuals who are either LGBT or disabled are more likely to be discriminated against or not have access to the support they need.

Naturally, it also depends on what part of 'BAME' they come from, for example, a BAME LGBT+ individual who comes from a country that has more liberalised views (e.g., Japan) is less likely to face as many issues as someone from another country where being anything other than straight is culturally taboo or illegal. Most individuals from BAME backgrounds will probably come from a country that has hostile views.

I find it easiest to conceptualise intersectionality as the movement to understand the nuances of a large group better. In other words, moving towards the realisation that 'women', 'disabled' 'BAME' or 'LGBT+' are not homogenous groups, an individual's life experience or personal circumstance can dramatically shift how they have experienced the world.

Understanding diversity

In my previous workplace, we looked to better address the issue of BAME women by bringing together our race network with our women's network as a joint initiative. This way we could benefit from the understanding that people from ethnic minority backgrounds had a particular experience, whilst the women's network could highlight issues that women face. I would be less familiar with certain issues as a male, such as pressures around having children, maternity leave, and issues of returning to work.

By building this connection we could gain a better picture of the issues faced and build more coherent approaches to improve the situation. Naturally, this group needed to be also actually run by BAME women, as it would have been problematic to have it run solely by BAME men and white women.

I see intersectionality as a positive trend. Whilst I do believe that using terms like 'BAME' or 'LGBT+' has its uses, it also has its limits. By bringing together the different characteristics of an individual, it helps us understand their experiences better. This approach also allows a more granular approach that goes past such larger labels but also does not go so in-depth that it becomes impossible to build an evidence base.

There is a temptation for us to stop using any of these terms and refer to ourselves simply as 'people' due to how different we are. But I feel this would become too intangible and would lead to leaving inclusion issues unaddressed. After all, if pregnant women are being looked over for promotion consistently, then we ought to address that.

Why 'inclusion'?

In this book, I have frequently accompanied the concept of diversity with inclusion.

Inclusion is the idea that people can fully contribute to the environment that they are in. In the workplace, this means being able to contribute to wider strategies, planning, and decisions about their work and how things work, no matter who they are or what they think. This is based upon a general level of mutual respect and valuing of each member of a team. This is often underpinned by a team charter.

Inclusion matters because diversity on its own does little to change things. Historically, many diversity programmes focussed purely on the metrics – ensuring that they hired more women or BAME staff to shift the numbers.

What happened was that many staff from these backgrounds joined the workplace, but rather than being hired to genuinely contribute or provide their experiences, they were quickly told to conform to the systems that had already been created. These systems were not made for people like them, and as such, they found themselves less included and welcomed by their organisations. These staff would be one of the first to leave.

We saw this a few decades ago for women. The career ladder was created for those that worked hardest, stayed the latest in the office and were the most visible. Attendance at the Friday evening pub drinks was mandatory. The idea of an individual not going to the social (which incidentally had a very macho environment) or needing to pause their careers for having children was paramount to career suicide. Unfortunately, women would naturally be far more likely to have caring responsibilities than a man. They were therefore quickly faced with the choice of whether to focus on their career or having a family. Whilst times have changed, this issue is still very relevant, and is one of the reasons why we see so few women on boards of organisations.

Another example of poor integration is with BAME staff. Often, BAME staff have been brought in at the bottom of the organisation, either through a diversity internship scheme or in operational roles. Whilst this has improved the diversity of the organisation statistically, there is little chance for them to rise through the ranks due to a lack of opportunity or support. The organisation can point to having a good percentage of BAME staff, but on inspection, few to none are in positions of decision-making authority.

With inclusion though, these staff can feel more comfortable contributing in the same way as other members of staff. In the short term, this allows more junior staff to have a voice in what their organisation does. In the longer term, it equalises disparities and allows junior staff from underrepresented groups to rise in the organisation at the same rate as more privileged colleagues. In other words, by building a better culture of inclusion, we are aiming to improve disparities of statistics that these groups have, such as lower engagement, performance scores, and the likelihood of promotion.

From a business perspective, more diversity without inclusion can lead to worse performance outcomes, rather than better ones. In an environment where little inclusion happens, by adding people from different backgrounds, we are more likely to create divisive groups and disgruntled staff members who feel overlooked. This leads to unhappiness, lower productivity, and higher turnover.

Diversity *with* inclusion makes the most of difference of opinion and thoughts, actively bringing them into the conversation and better decision-making. This capitalises on the benefits and leads to higher productivity levels and financial outcomes that we previously mentioned in the business case data.

Unfortunately, inclusion is very hard to measure. However, just like any idea of 'culture' or 'team spirit', whilst it is hard to quantify, it can be felt. We all know environments where we have been welcomed and made to feel a part of a group, as well as many more times where we have felt the opposite. Where we feel welcome, we feel able to relax more, give our honest views, enjoy the company of others, and feel valued. When we do not, we usually feel insecure, aloof, and less happy.

I would probably guess that we've also been in environments that we enjoy, but others have complained about not being particularly welcoming. We are often surprised, as we enjoy that place or group, whereas they do not as they perhaps complain it as 'cliquey' or not welcoming for someone like them. For me, this has often been when out with other males, whereas females may have found the conversation crass or sexist – I certainly remember a lot of that in my teenage years!

Our aim with inclusion is to build a feeling of being welcomed but ensure that it is for everyone, rather than a certain group of people. Naturally, it is harder to see when a group is not inclusive if we feel included within it.

We will explore ways in which to build greater inclusion within this book, but essentially this relates to building a culture where people are welcomed and there is an openness to different thoughts and ideas.

This relies on breaking down ingrained ways of working which can include an overreliance on hierarchy, insecurity of people in their jobs, or a culture of being 'busy' where time for open conversations is non-existent. A culture of inclusion is a way of being that we embody in our actions every day.

What are 'equity' and the 'diamond rule'?

You may find other people using similar terminology: a new trend is also to additionally talk about 'equity' – looking at equality of outcomes by removing barriers for all. The idea of this is to better examine the issues that people face and create measures to overcome them.

This idea moves further than 'equality' which is looking to treat everyone the same.

To give a practical example, equality would be telling all staff members that they will have the same rights, no matter their situation or background. Equity would be giving additional flexibility to a pregnant woman by allowing them reasonable adjustments to work from home more often.

Equity makes both business and moral sense because by giving the pregnant woman more flexibility, her ability to do her job is higher, and her satisfaction as an employee is higher as it better suits her needs. This has added benefits for the team who have a colleague who spends fewer days sick. Focussing on equality would prevent these benefits, as a manager would be overly concerned about whether it was 'fair' that one person was able to work from home more than the rest of the team.

In practice, when there is a good and supportive environment, employees will tend to support an employer that makes adjustments for their colleagues. This shows employees are valued by the organisation, and if they were to ever be in a similar situation (e.g., sick leave) they could expect compassion from their organisation. Unfortunately, managers can often miss this point for fear of being seen to give preferential treatment.

The idea of equality can also perpetuate unhelpful views – an often-used phrase when discussing race is that people 'do not see colour'.

Unless they are literally colour-blind, people see colour! The issue with this is that it often ends up shutting down the conversation, or issues that individuals from BAME backgrounds want to raise. It is very hard to argue that something is a problem (e.g., statistically far lower performance markings) if you are speaking to someone who says they cannot see it. From my experience, this answer is often used predominantly (but not exclusively) by white individuals, who are well-meaning but still looking at these issues from an outdated perspective.

I believe this partly stems from what it used to be 'right' to say, as the idea of seeing colour made it sound like you were actively discriminating against them. However, when broken down the analogy makes little sense. To take a counter-example, we know people's gender (notwithstanding a small number of individuals who do not identify with either). If we were in a corridor and the men's toilets were on the left and the women's toilets were on the right if a male asked me which toilet they should use I would not reply to them 'I do not see gender'.

Not recognising that I have a skin colour also negates my life experiences in several different ways. For example, it infers that I do not have a rich family heritage that includes parents and grandparents that were born outside of the UK. This negates a whole topic of conversation. In practice, this can feel quite exclusionary.

I recall starting my job at the same time as a white colleague. He was asked all about his family background and his accent as he was from Newcastle. The rest of the team did not feel comfortable asking me about my background. So, despite joining on the same day at the same grade, I felt far less included than my white peer.

Another diversity concept that is worth knowing is the 'Diamond Rule'. You may have heard of the 'Golden Rule' – treat others how you would like to be treated yourself. Naturally, this is a good way of building empathy, but it is limited in its ability to fully understand the experience of others that shape the way they may want to be treated.

The Diamond Rule is that you treat others how *they* would like to be treated. In other words, not presuming what they may or may not want, instead actually asking them. In practice, this is asking things like whether they prefer their name to be abbreviated or not and asking their working preferences.

Understanding diversity

To give a very literal example, there are seats in the London Underground that have priority for those who have difficulty standing. I must confess I often sit in these seats as they are near the door (though in my defence, I do so when I am doubtful anyone is going to sit there!) Now, if an elderly person were to walk in, I am sure we have all experienced that slightly awkward situation of not being sure whether we should stand up at the risk of being presumptuous that this person cannot walk well, or doing nothing and being a selfish, terrible person.

I usually ask the individual if they would like my seat. Sometimes they say yes, and sometimes they say no. This allows that person to make the choice and avoids embarrassment if I were to assume they would need it. This is an example of me putting their needs first, rather than me deciding what is right for them. It is much better to ask someone what they would prefer then presuming and getting it totally wrong.

It reminds me of an old tale with a former manager. When she asked how I was during one of my one-on-one meetings, I told her that I had a friend commit suicide recently. She said 'yeah…' and then moved on to talk about work. I felt this was insensitive and lacked basic decency. I later brought this up with her. She replied that she had assumed that I did not want to talk about the subject at all! This highlights how people making assumptions can have serious negative effects on relationships and wellbeing of staff.

What we mean by privilege

A term you may have come across when delving into the world of diversity is 'privilege'.

From my experience, this is the term that emits the most hostility, perhaps because it has been used or received in an accusatory way. I personally do not believe it ought to be used as a critique, but more of a concept to better understand different life experiences, where some have benefited from opportunities or faced greater challenges.

I am not in the game of criticising people for who they are or looking to guilt trip people for being fortunate in having a good upbringing. This is to highlight that these advantages do exist so that it becomes more apparent to us all what differences it can make to have certain privileges compared to those that did not.

In terms of a definition, privilege is the idea of having an advantage which is only available to a certain group or person. It is most used in the sense of 'white privilege'; essentially highlighting the fact that white individuals are far less likely to face certain day-to-day barriers than BAME people do; the reason we use this concept is that it is sometimes not evident that these privileges exist, as we often believe that others generally would have the same experience as us.

I once returned to the UK with my British Passport with a group of other university students from a trip to France. When looking at my passport, I was told 'this isn't you, is it?'. Whilst I explained I was part of a trip and managed to pass through, I found it a shocking experience. I felt unwelcomed back to my own country because I had a foreign-sounding name. No other white person on the trip was questioned about the validity of their passport.

I cannot say that this would never happen to a white person, and yet it did not happen to them. When I told this experience to a group of white people, they were shocked, whereas when I said it to BAME individuals they tended to have experienced something similar. Considering this has happened to me several times, it gave me the sense that I am a second-class citizen compared to my white colleagues. These small actions can have a knock-on effect in terms of my own self-esteem, which also built personal insecurities of being different compared to my peers.

Privilege is not just about skin colour. It can also be about the wider advantages we face in life. This can often get quite complex, as whilst we may have benefitted in one area, we may have been disadvantaged in others.

To take myself as an example, I was fortunate enough to go to a fee-paying school, where I had many opportunities to do several extracurricular activities. I had a tutor who proofread my university application, ultimately leading me to be accepted, where I could do a year abroad in France. Whilst the activities I did were indeed done by me, the fact I had attended a school which gave me numerous advantages was not my achievement. Rather it was the financial success of my parents which allowed them to send me to a highly reputable school.

At the same time, I found school difficult, as one of the very few brown faces in a predominantly white, Christian school. I also had the difficulties of being across two cultures, which made it hard for me to feel like I fit in within either culture. Whilst I may have felt more British, my family emphasised that my true home was Bangladesh. In school, I had a foreign name and a different skin colour.

I found growing up in a school surrounded by white children difficult, and yet still benefitted from this privilege that set me up later in life. So, it is important to understand this experience for yourself, what benefits you may have had and also the difficulties.

There will be activities later in this book that will help you better understand this for yourself.

II.   Human behaviour and our ecosystem

Understanding human behaviour is critical for us to understand why many of the issues that we see are so prevalent across organisations. Many of the issues around diversity are based on how we act as individuals, and how we are hardwired to act. For example, we often see similar issues of BAME employees feeling segregated and 'othered', with other staff treating them differently to their colleagues. I certainly have felt this personally, even when it is done inadvertently or unconsciously. So, by understanding more about how we behave, we can better understand the issues that we face.

I find it incredibly useful to bring a coaching perspective into the conversation around diversity. This will give you a wider understanding of how we act as humans and how that can, at times, get us into issues. You may have come across many of the points I bring up before, perhaps through a leadership workshop or from wider reading. Nonetheless, it is always beneficial to further examine them, particularly in the context of your own journey around better understanding diversity for you.

How we rationalise things as humans

We as humans are fascinating and complicated.

One individual will react to one situation in one way, having taken in all the stimuli around them. Another individual will then reason in an opposite way. For example, many of us go to the cinema to see a movie. Despite watching the same film, two people can have completely different views on how they found it. Both people can have completely reasonable arguments which follow 'rational' logic. But how can they both be right about the film if we are to search for objective truth? There is so much that is both very rational, but also very irrational about us.

Many of us working in organisations learn to speak about things in an evidence-based, methodological way. This likely considers the different options, risks, and opportunities. Equally, we have tastes or preferences in things like film, music and food which are completely subjective and very hard to explain logically. The world of 'rational', professional work and the subjective way in which we operate in our lives are far closer than we think.

To take a very mundane example, we can be tired in the evening when we still have work to complete. We can logically argue to ourselves that as we are tired, we should leave it to the morning when we have more energy, and rest for the evening. Equally, we can argue to ourselves that we should complete this task tonight so that we have a less hectic morning the next day. Which one is the correct decision?

Perhaps we follow what we are generally told, in that procrastination is bad, so it is better to complete it tonight to get it over and done with. But what if that leads us to complete the task poorly because we were tired, and we would have been better off doing it the next morning?

Equally, if we decided to do this tomorrow and did not complete this task tonight, what if something came up tomorrow morning that we could not foresee, preventing us from completing it?

Perhaps you may be thinking that these options are too binary, and another option would be to do the work tonight and check it over the next morning, which equally sounds sensible.

The point though is that there is not a right or wrong in any of these situations.

Now I want you to think of someone, a colleague or friend who was in this situation. If they were to ask them what their plans are for completing this task if they stated it was any of the three options above, would you do much else other than say that the plan seems sensible?

The point of this example is to highlight that our brains have a magnificent ability to rationalise many different decisions. There are so many variables and different considerations we could make, that we can feasibly convince ourselves that any one of these things is the 'right' answer if we spend enough time telling ourselves that is the case.

We do this to bring some level of decision-making into our lives. Without the ability to judge subjective information or things we do not know; we would be stuck forever unable to make the most basic of decisions in our lives.

The issue is when we believe that our answer or point of view is the only decision or the 'done' thing. If we have spent our lifetime being told that we need to complete our work and not procrastinate, we would assume that this would be the natural right answer. What this does not consider is how other people's personal preferences may be very different, or that they grew up with the opposite view.

Naturally, this is a relatively unimportant situation that is unlikely to have large-scale differences in how you perceive individuals. However, when brought into the context of a character judgement, it can support our views in judging people who do things differently as suspiciously, whilst those who do things similarly as more normal.

It is why there are so vehement debates on relatively trivial things. In the UK, we often argue whether jam comes before or after cream on a scone (I tend to vehemently argue for one side, but then forget which one I support the next time I am asked). We would cry in disgust at the idea of people putting milk into their tea before water. There are also many other examples we have seen, such as the phenomenon on the internet of people arguing whether 'The Dress' was either black and blue or white and gold. (If you missed this, simply search 'The Dress' on the internet and judge for yourself).

Human behaviour and our ecosystem

The reason this matters is to highlight that we see the world subjectively and that we can rationalise pretty much any standpoint. Whilst we may believe our viewpoint of the world to be the correct one, we can make these judgements without having any evidence of it being true.

Within the context of work, we also have a natural tendency to prefer our own way of doing things and look for this when speaking with others, for example in arguments, we regularly look for people who agree with us. What this means is that we have an inherent preference, or bias, for those who make similar judgements, and an inhibition against those who make different judgements.

This also touches upon how we are socially programmed – we much prefer people who are going to agree with us than ones who disagree with us. I believe that this is due to how our social system of education teaches us that success is based upon being liked, and we constantly search for the approval of our teachers and parents. This crosses into our habits and continues into the way we operate at work.

In practice, this means that our human tendencies are to prefer similarity over the difference. When talking about diversity, this is one of the major obstacles that underlines why such issues occur. Sometimes there is a temptation to assume that there are no problems because no one is actively discriminating.

Unfortunately, we often find that cliques form in a workplace anyway.

What is 'bias'?

Examining bias is a critical part of diversity and inclusion. This may have been a term you have also heard previously.

Bias is the concept behind us having certain preferences – either good or bad – against certain people or things.

The important thing to underline is that we all have biases, in some form or another. Our upbringing, social interactions and influences all shape how we view and see the world. What makes these difficult to identify is that these are often **unconscious**, meaning that we have a bias in one way or another, but we do not realise that this is the case.

This often makes raising the subject of biases with individuals quite difficult. A quite normal response from a lot of people would be to state that they do not hold any biases and that they view and treat everybody the same.

Sometimes this is stated as a defiant reaction towards the subject of diversity and inclusion as deliberately defensive, but often it is through a genuine belief that they, as an individual have no biases. Whilst it would be great if that were the case, unfortunately, it's not true!

The Harvard Implicit Association Test illustrates this well – this is a free online test you can do which looks at how your initial reactions link people of certain characteristics to certain professions or stories. I would recommend you give this a go if you have the time – it is freely available online and will tell you more about your own biases. You can find it by searching for it online.

If you do not believe me, then I will share a snapshot of my own results. Despite coming from an ethnic minority background, I tend to prefer white individuals and have a negative preference for others who are ethnic minorities.

Surprisingly, the trend for young people also follows this, which I theorise as the proliferation of negative messaging through social media. With younger people consuming more content than ever before, any negative stereotypes of individuals are reinforced to a greater degree than ever before.

Biases matter because they can greatly affect our decision-making. In a business environment, this is particularly prominent in recruitment and promotion. We expect people to fit a certain mould, so when they do not, we implicitly feel they may not be suitable for a role or opportunity.

In practice, those who state they are not biased, do not see colour, or always treat people equally tend to be the people who are more likely to commit biased actions. It is also difficult to point this out to them, as they return to the point that they have treated everyone equally so cannot be biased. This means there is no conversation about how they might mitigate any biases, which is particularly important for areas such as recruitment panels.

We often see this in higher profile cases of racism or sexism in the media, where the response from the accused tends to be a flat-out denial by simply reiterating that they are not a racist, sexist, homophobe etc. This is often followed by an 'I am sorry that you were offended by this!'. For the communities that are affected by these remarks, this often feels hollow and defensive.

To take a simple example, imagine a typical nurse working in a hospital. Now I would like you to imagine a doctor. If you were like me, the image that comes to me is that the nurse is a woman, and a doctor is a man. We are therefore more predisposed to come to a hospital to be greeted by a female nurse and be administered by a male doctor.

Whilst things may be changing that we are more accustomed to seeing female doctors, being greeted by a male nurse may still be a bit of a shock to the system. From the point of view of the nurse though, they may feel more resistance from you compared to their female counterparts, making their job harder. They may also be questioned more by friends and family about their career choice.

Conversely, women who are in roles where they are not traditionally represented such as in construction are far more likely to be questioned about their competence than their male counterparts.

In offices with a particularly imbalanced gender divide, this can often mean that women are not visible in senior leadership positions. A culture can quickly build up that leadership traits are those exhibited by men and not those by women. This tends to play out within performance management meetings where there is a notable difference in the way in which men and women are assessed, despite this being an 'objective' process.

For example, a man may be seen as assertive and confident within a meeting; however, a woman may often get the critique that if they acted similarly that they were aggressive, bossy, or bitchy. Furthermore, a male dominant office may have a certain cultural norm of machismo and bravado, something that a woman will always find more difficult to flourish in.

What compounds this bias is that not only do we have negative biases against those who tend to be different to us, but we tend to also have preferential biases for those like us.

So, on top of the additional difficulty of a woman being more harshly judged than her male counterparts, if the manager is also a male, he may naturally lean towards the male he manages rather than the female. This is because he may have more in common; for example, an interest in sports.

Even if the female also is interested in the sport, the manager may assume that this is an improper conversation with a woman so does not bring it up, meaning a weaker rapport with her compared to the male colleague. It also might just simply be that this male manager is more comfortable speaking with another male rather than a female, meaning the other male becomes the 'go-to' person for exciting work.

There are several things to look out for in a recruitment panel or discussion around performances. Phrases such as 'I see myself in him', or 'I was just like that at his age' can sometimes be an indication of an inert preference for that person due to the identification of their journey.

Whilst there is nothing wrong with this individually, it may lead to a preference for this person purely because they have a perceived similar life journey compared to another candidate.

Bias is a large and complex topic, so there are also more examples and details that you could explore outside of this book. The important point though is that you understand that this is relevant to you.

No one is judging you for having biases, because to have biases is to be human! However, the only way to actively mitigate them is to first understand that these exist.

Blind spots and how we perceive ourselves

Each of us has our own blind spots. From our current point of view, there are certain areas that we cannot see. This is not evident to us because we cannot see them.

An example of a blind spot is when you cannot see a particular action or behaviour you exhibit, even if this is something evident to people around you.

Blind spots are particularly important when relating to diversity and inclusion as these are often behaviours related to how we work with different people. If you are not used to working with women, LGBT+ staff or an ethnic minority you may implicitly feel more uncertain around them and how to react.

I have heard several instances of managers fearing being seen as discriminatory or racist against their BAME staff. As such they avoid giving feedback to them. In practice, this leads to the BAME staff getting less support in their jobs compared with their white peers, and often feeling like they do not have a proper line of communication with their managers. This perpetuates the issue of BAME staff not getting promoted within the organisation.

For a more explicit example, I recall starting a job in a new team. On reflection, it was not a particularly well-oiled or inclusive team. I noted the head of team who was a white woman did not give me a welcome when I started, whereas when a white (and more junior) colleague joined a week later, she got a hearty welcome from the head of team who was delighted for them to be joining. This new colleague had previously worked with the head of team.

The head of team seemed to be uncomfortable speaking with me directly. It was a bit bizarre, but she was not looking me in the eye when she spoke. Instead, she would always be looking at something or someone else. I noticed she did not do this with anyone else.

I did raise this as an issue at one point. However, my head of team denied that this was the case and that I must be mistaken as she was sure she did not deliberately do anything of the sort. I left feeling disillusioned. I did not decide to raise it as a bigger issue as ultimately it was my word against that of my boss.

In these instances, it can feel like perhaps we are mistaken. However, at one point another ethnic minority member of staff approached me and told me outright 'You know you are treated differently compared to the other managers, right?'.

The tricky thing about blind spots is that you will rarely hear people telling you about your own. There are likely things you do not know about yourself, but other people do. it takes a particularly open and inclusive culture – built upon psychological safety (which we will visit in the next chapter) for people to feel able to genuinely tell you what they think.

It also takes a strength of character for an individual to be truly open to hearing the views of different members of staff and allow them to give such views frankly without fear of reprimand. Such openness to challenge is rare from leaders.

Organisations often try to build feedback into their performance management systems; this can be '360-feedback', i.e., feedback that has come from your boss, your peers, your reports, and wider stakeholders you are involved in. This is to give a greater picture of what you do, and how you are perceived by your colleagues. This can be a helpful exercise for bringing up issues, particularly when it is anonymised.

In theory, this can solve the problem, though from my experience this can be hit-and-miss. I have previously been asked to do 360-feedback as part of a performance measure. I would also ask for 360-feedback from this person as well, meaning I would avoid saying something negative in case they would do the same for me.

Once, my manager told me to do a 360-feedback exercise. I later learnt that although he was also doing 360-feedback, he had deliberately not asked me for feedback but had asked my peers. This was despite me being his direct line manage. They knew I was critical of certain parts of their leadership so omitted me from the exercise.

I complained about this and brought it up the chain as highlighting the flaw behind a diversity and inclusion strategy when such practices were commonplace. First, my head of team looked to play down the issue, stating that it was perhaps an administrative error and that I was welcome to give feedback outside of the process anyway. I had to go to an external colleague to complain and highlight the flaw in the system.

The solution was that a new rule was put in that 360-feedback must include people you are managed by within the directorate. But my manager faced no negative repercussions or punishment. Furthermore, I later learned that I was the only member of staff being told that I should do 360-degree feedback, with other colleagues at my level not being told to do so.

360-feedback can work to reveal our blind spots when they are for development, rather than a performance review. When the mindset is about development rather than proving you deserve a pay rise, the approach is very different.

Aside from anonymised feedback, my personal preference is for leaders to reinforce a culture of feedback throughout the process. This means asking their reports and stakeholders regularly what they think and how they can improve. It is also helpful to go to trusted confidants and ask more in-depth questions about their genuine views.

The key to this is asking consistently so that it feels normal for the person you are asking. Be aware that the person being asked will likely feel uncomfortable saying what they really think, usually from a general office culture of reprisal against disagreeing with the boss, or just common courtesy and not wanting to say anything negative to your face. It is important to ask a few times and ideally be quite specific in the ask.

This means asking about how you performed as a presenter in a meeting, rather than how people find you in general. People can be wary of being asked for feedback out of the blue, or expect that this is simply a corporate ask that is a tick-box exercise.

This means they may raise rather bland feedback. If you've gone through a 360-feedback process before, I am sure you know exactly what I am talking about. I am certainly guilty of doing the same thing! Here is the sort of thing we tend to send:

'Jim is a nice guy and I find him a good person to work with. I like spending time with him as a colleague and he approaches things well.'

However, there is a way to get more effective feedback. For example, if you have just completed a presentation, you may find yourself asking others how they think it went. They will likely give general impressions that it went well. You could then follow up by asking if there was anything particularly good, or that you could improve. Alternatively, you could give your views and see whether it correlates to what the other person thinks. 'I thought point x might have been a bit long-winded, what do you think?'

Of course, not everyone will have some great deep insight, so it's important to ask several different people that you come into contact with throughout your day. Over time, you will likely find people who are more confident in giving their views, including constructive feedback, compared to others.

As someone who would fit themselves in the category of willing to give feedback (I do not mind being known as the person who can tell the hard truths!), I would emphasise that it is important to be grateful that someone dares to give their honest views. Any overtly negative reaction from yourself will likely lead to people never raising their voices again!

Unfortunately, many organisations complain about nobody being willing to raise their hands when faced with a challenge when those same organisations actively discourage different opinions when they do not fit the view of leadership.

Another way to explore blind spots is to work with a coach. If you have not worked with a coach before, this is an opportunity for you to bring forward an issue or challenge you are facing.

By taking time to properly explore the issue, along with prompts and guidance from a coach, you will find you can better understand some of the actions and why you think people are reacting in different ways to your own actions. Done over a series of sessions, it can be an extremely powerful way to better understand yourself, what works well, and what is causing any issues that you cannot see.

When I work with clients as their coach, I take the time to establish a healthy social contract – we are equals, meaning they are committed to listening to the reflections I give them, and I am in a position that can challenge their thinking if necessary. Coaching is not all about challenging though, more often it is a safe space of trust where individuals can explore the doubts or discomfort, they have on broaching certain subjects.

When coaching individuals around diversity and inclusion, the issues raised in this book such as the different terminology can be blockers. Other people were worried about being a 'white saviour', which whilst well intentioned was preventing them from taking any action at all. Through a series of sessions, these issues can be tackled which allows for greater clarity of thought and performance.

Building psychological safety

In the corporate workplace, we are rarely in mortal danger. Unless we are in a frontline emergency service role, we are probably not particularly worried about whether we are going to survive at the end of each day.

However, our brains do not see this distinction. Brains react to danger in a similar way when we are threatened psychologically as when we are threatened physically. In an office setting, we often have impending deadlines which can give us a sense of impending doom, Many of us have found ourselves attending meetings which get heated due to dramatic clashes of ideas.

There are many dysfunctional workplaces which are characterised by pressure and insecurity. Team members are constantly trying to prove themselves, and they may spend more time worrying about saying the right thing to their bosses than doing the job. In this space, the main priority for an employee is survival. This leads to avoiding giving opinions or disagreeing with the manager, rather than coming up with creative solutions.

There is a part of our brain called the amygdala which is our fight-or-flight sensor.[12] This will kick in when we feel threatened. The amygdala is our human instinct to react to danger and respond accordingly. Historically we would rely on this to face or flee a danger such as a wild animal coming to attack us.

Unfortunately, in the modern workplace, this response leads us to often lose sensory control and flare up. If you have ever found yourself losing your temper and saying something you regret, it is probably your amygdala which has taken over your senses. This is often described as 'seeing red', and is why people may blow up over an argument. Others may simply freeze, with the hope that this will let the situation pass without any further negative repercussions.

For diversity, an insecure environment is not ideal for obvious reasons – as we highlighted in the last chapter, a workplace that is not inclusive is unlikely to be enjoyed by all. However, on top of this, workplace pressure is likely to lead to a

---

[12] Daniel Kahnemen, *Thinking Fast and Slow* (2011), p.301

worse environment due to a sense of insecurity. For an individual from a minority, the effect is usually heightened. They are likely to feel even less secure than their counterparts.

Daniel Kahneman's book 'Thinking Fast and Slow'[13] broadly defines our thinking as 'System 1' and 'System 2' – System 1 is our faster response, which is quicker and necessary when facing immediate danger, but is far more prone to biased thinking. System 2 on the other hand is when we slow down and take more time to assess. This allows us to critically think, and whilst it does not mean there will be no bias whatsoever, it does allow us to critically examine whether we may have been making implicit and unfair assumptions.

In an insecure or toxic environment, we are far more likely to be defensive and revert to System 1 thinking, which from a diversity perspective means we are relying far more on pre-judgements. Women may be presumed to be too emotional to deal with a tough situation. A BAME or disabled staff member may be assumed to not have the capability to handle a piece of work.

When working in pressurised environments, quick decisions are made to keep up with the necessary demands. As a younger member of staff, I have often been in the office later due to no childcare requirements. I was given the stretching piece of work which benefitted my career, as I was literally in front of my manager at the right place at the right time.

On the other hand, I have also seen at a separate point my job being side-lined as I was presumed to not be able to handle the more prominent and demanding parts of the role. My manager presumed that I was not interested in the more difficult tasks. I found myself stuck in a cycle of being seen to be ineffective whilst having very few real opportunities to change that narrative. This was tough for me to handle. At the time, this affected my sense of self-worth. With hindsight, I realised this was me relying on the judgment of others to determine how I saw myself.

---

[13] Daniel Kahnemen, *Thinking Fast and Slow* (2011)

From a business perspective, psychological safety is one of the key elements to success. A study of Google's most successful teams found that the top key dynamic was psychological safety.[14] Individuals can suggest risks or areas of improvement without feeling exposed for doing so.

It allowed for higher performance by giving the space to make mistakes, and later learn from them. This is a very different approach to one where we feel we must get it 'right' the first time. Amy Edmondson's book 'The Fearless Organization: Creating Psychological Safety in the Workplace for Learning, Innovation, and Growth' is also particularly influential in this area.

Psychological safety also supports wider diversity initiatives of making a team more open and honest in terms of their personal lives. For example, a space where a gay individual can come out can greatly reduce their need to keep their personal life hidden from colleagues, leading to higher engagement, wellbeing, and happiness. This also applies to other minority groups.

Psychological safety can be created by building greater space for honest conversations and an ability for people to give their opinions without reprimand. It also is built based upon trust – if you as a leader are promising better working conditions, it is important that you deliver this, as otherwise, your staff will not trust you in your promises.

I have previously heard in one of my previous roles about the aim of building a 'listening culture'. Ironically, after this was announced this was the first and last time I heard anything further about it. Empty promises have a limited shelf-life and can do more harm than good.

---

[14] https://rework.withgoogle.com/blog/five-keys-to-a-successful-google-team/

In-groups and out-groups

As humans, we often have the desire to fit in. Think back to school, and how we desired the commonality of friendship and being a part of a wider group.

This is a natural part of the human experience. It also plays a key part in how we develop. Think back to your friendship group when you were younger – how did this influence you? Perhaps it exposed you to things you may not have otherwise. I had a friend who was strongly into photography as a hobby, and as such, I was exposed to the world of photography which I probably would not have passed by otherwise.

Most of my friends were white. I remember the discomfort and shyness I had when speaking with their parents, as I had an innate understanding that parents were authority figures, rather than there being a relatively open relationship between parent and child. I remember once being invited to a friend's for dinner, and when his mum asked if I wanted some additional pizza toppings I was too shy to say yes.

The experience made me realise what I had in my family was not the norm for everyone else. The groups that we spend time around can greatly dictate how we see the world, and what we see the 'norm' as being.

In diversity literature, we talk about 'in-groups' and 'out-groups'. Think of a football match, or pretty much any sporting event. Naturally, we see groups of fans cheering on their team in a highly partisan way. If you were to attend a sporting event, you may wear the colours of your team. You might pass a stranger or sit next to someone also wearing the same colours and immediately have a connection as being part of one side.

This connection feels very nice as it makes us feel like we belong as a part of a wider group. It is nice to have people around us who are on the same side, and it can be pretty affirming of our views.

Now, think about how you might clash with someone from the *other* side. Perhaps you may pass someone wearing the opposition colours, you may feel a sense of hesitancy, and depending on how strongly it matters to you, you may feel the desire to keep your distance.

I am sure that if you follow a sports team you are perfectly able to be friends with people who support the opposition. You may clash with them on matchday, but otherwise, you can have a perfectly normal relationship.

This is an illustrative snapshot of what we mean by an in-group and an out-group. The example of a football match is helpful because it demonstrates this point so clearly. It is also quite remarkable to a neutral at how riled up the different sides can get, and how different they can perceive a subjective occurrence (such as a referee's decision to call a foul).

We no doubt have experienced this in some way at school. Think of the cliques illustrated within movies such as Mean Girls, where there is a set of popular kids and those who are not. Nothing epitomises this better than the rather iconic line of 'you can't sit with us'.

In the workplace, we tend to work with a relatively small amount of people. Often, you might not know each other that well. This will likely lead you to approach the person who feels most accessible to speak to, and that person is likely someone who has a similarity to you.

This natural tendency can quickly build an 'in-group' mentality. The group tends to keep to themselves, make decisions and deliberately exclude those that they think do not fit with them. An example of this would be a part of the team having lunch together but only inviting a select set of people, and deliberately avoiding others whilst doing so.

At this lunch, it may be an opportunity to complain about the other colleagues. If it is with people who directly work with one another, it might even be a place where work decisions are made. This means that those outside of the group are left out of a key component of work, even if their job role means that they should be consulted.

We have likely seen and experienced this at some point in our lives. The individual from the outside sees this as being part of the 'out-group'. In other words, this individual is deliberately excluded from social activities, and in particularly bad instances, this spills over into actual work where they are not consulted.

This is not a particularly fun experience. It can be quite awkward and uncomfortable to find your team having lunch without you, or hearing about it through gossip. Over time it can have led to feeling unhappy, being less engaged with work and a drop in morale.

I recall at one workplace hearing about some social gathering. However, it was strongly emphasised that this was a gathering that had a 'No Men' policy. I did not particularly care to attend it anyway, but there was something quite striking about someone saying directly that they were having a social gathering and that I was not allowed to be there.

From a diversity lens, this 'othering' happens a lot. Often, BAME, women, disabled staff, or pretty much anyone who might be seen as 'different' (e.g., has a different accent) find themselves being less likely to be included in a conversation. This often puts them under additional pressure to fit in. They often feel the need to hide certain aspects of themselves.

To take the example of women, this has often meant not wanting to raise issues with inappropriate issues in the workplace, as they do not want to risk their hard-earned status of being included. Other women who are seen to complain about such behaviour can be ostracised for not being a 'good sport'.

Understanding in-group and out-group behaviour is critical to better comprehending some of the more subjective issues around diversity. Whilst it may sound petty and small, it can be as big as the difference as one employee describing the employer as the best place they've ever worked for, or why a member of staff leaves in under 12 months after starting.

The scary and confusing part of this is that both realities may be occurring simultaneously. in other words, a white person may describe the group as welcoming and a great place to work, however from a BAME employee's eyes they feel uncomfortable due to the number of inappropriate comments.

It is why we talk so much about the need for genuine inclusion within the workplace. Whilst in-group behaviour is a natural tendency, the aim of building greater inclusion is to actively counteract some of the negative consequences that can be created by this.

The tone is often set by the leader, and the culture that has built up in the group is implicitly likely to be based on what they see as normal.

I will also emphasise that in-group and out-groups can happen in any situation, I have been in south Asian-dominated groups where I was part of the in-group. There was clear hostile regard to women. Equally, I have been in the opposite situation of being the out-group as the BAME male in a group dominated by white women. What we are talking about is the way our mind works as humans, rather than the characteristic of any group.

There are ways to address this. For example, actively including new members of staff or creating an invitation that is open to all within a workplace as a default rule. People appreciate when they are included, and this greatly improved their wellbeing within the workplace.

We can also take time to actively review who we are including in meetings and social situations. This can ensure that we are not defaulting to the people who we are most comfortable with. Instead, we can ensure people who should be in the conversation are included.

Group think

You may be finding that you are surrounded by people who might be like you. This means that in the grander scale of things, you are not getting a true breadth of ideas and perspectives when you are making a decision. This is referred to as 'group think'.

If you are deciding for your organisation and neglect to invite the whole of the marketing team, there probably will be issues that arise later down the line. This applies to diversity issues as well. As we have highlighted previously, a wider set of backgrounds within a team means that people can call upon different life experiences when brainstorming ideas.

For example, younger staff can be much more in touch with the latest popular culture than older staff (in general), despite them being more likely to be junior members of staff. Going through social media can demonstrate which companies have embraced the importance of understanding shifting cultural change. Whilst some companies release quirky posts, there are still companies that write posts as if they were a formal letter.

Following the invasion of Iraq, an independent inquiry was held in the UK, colloquially known as the Chilcot Inquiry.[15] The report highlighted decision-making within Government as a major failure, due to the propensity for group think decision-making.

The starting assumption was that Saddam Hussein had Weapons of Mass Destruction (WMDs), and at no point was an attempt made to question this, nor consider the possibility that these WMDs had been disposed of. From this basis, the decision to invade was more convincing.

The brilliant minds within the UK Government did not question this basic assumption. This was even though it was a major reason for going to war which would affect millions of lives. However, these sorts of examples illustrate that

---

[15] https://www.gov.uk/government/publications/the-report-of-the-iraq-inquiry

even the largest of organisations with some of the smartest people and biggest resources fall into these fallacies.

Large organisations often fall into this trap as they feel like they have the 'greatest minds'. This means that there is a misconception that there is no possibility of human fallacy. However, no matter how brilliant people may be, they are still vulnerable to the same cognitive biases as we are. It is why decisions are more likely to be effective when they actively look to bring different views and are open to challenges.

If anything, smarter people can be more prone to this issue compared to those with relatively average intelligence. When intelligent people are so used to doing what their brain tells them, they can build up a sense of exceptionalism to the fallacies and biases of the brain. In other words, when you are used to generally being the smartest person in the room, you can condition yourself to be less open to challenge.

The positive side is that group think is far less likely to happen when we have already followed the different principles of inclusion and bringing greater diversity into our lives. Nonetheless, we should actively look to avoid making big decisions when only a certain type of people are within the room who are not representative of the wider population.

Unfortunately, stressful, and high-pressured environments are where these errors are most likely to occur. This is why it is critical to ensure proper time and due process takes place before making decisions and building a habit of following a proper process without falling into the temptation of cutting corners.

If you are in an organisation where procedures are routinely ignored or urgent work is often fast-tracked, remember that this is the place where the risk is at its greatest. The lessons from the Chilcot Inquiry demonstrate that this can happen at the highest level, to great human and economic cost. Take the oil spill in the Gulf of Mexico, for example. Rather than a technical failure, this was down to human failure in following agreed safety protocol. The total cost ended up being over 61 billion dollars.

Growth mindset and how it relates to diversity

You may be familiar with the concept of a Growth Mindset. Carol Dweck explains in her book 'Mindset' that a growth mindset is one where the individual believes that they can grow and learn.[16] People are not born in a single, static way. Instead, they develop. This is in contrast with those with a fixed mindset. If you have a fixed mindset, you generally believe that your traits are broadly static. In other words, you are born with a talent, or you are not.

Those who follow a growth mindset are more likely to grow and learn from their experiences. By picking up this book, you are learning more about a subject that you did not know about before, and through putting in the effort of self-education you can have a greater understanding of diversity and inclusion.

If, on the other hand, you approach this as a subject you already know everything about or one that you are unable to learn as it is beyond your capabilities, you are highly unlikely to get much out of reading this book.

Growth mindsets are also important when talking about diversity as it relates to how we see others and their ability to grow and succeed. In general, if you are a manager who believes in your staff's ability to improve, you will find it easier to give them stretching opportunities or new work.

This will give them greater job satisfaction and the ability to gain new skills. If, on the other hand, you have put your staff in a box as good at their job but not 'leadership material', you may be inadvertently holding a fixed mindset against that person.

For one reason or another, this situation tends to play out more often for ethnic minorities. I have seen many examples of ethnic minority staff joining the workforce and ending up working in less visible roles. They have become a trusted individual within the team due to their consistency and strong delivery. However, they are rarely viewed as people who are ready for a promotion.

---

[16] Carol Dweck, *Mindset: The New Psychology for Success* (2007)

They are often deemed as lacking leadership qualities, perhaps because they are not as vocal during meetings. Another frustrating issue is that the team feels like they could not afford to lose this person, due to their consistency within the team that underpins their success over a long period. As such, managers would prefer not to recommend them for promotion.

These may be valid concerns. However, it can often be seen as unfair when others do not face these same judgements, meaning people who are seen as having leadership qualities are promoted without having the same level of output or experience.

You may not directly manage BAME staff, women, or a disabled individual, however your colleagues might, or you may be the manager of someone who does. When having discussions about promotions and opportunities for development, this is a key opportunity to properly examine whether your team is fairly judging different people.

Are your colleagues making fair judgements about people's ability to grow and learn, or are they making assumptions relating to general stereotypes? Remember that there is also a tendency towards a bias towards people like us. This may be clouding your or your colleague's judgement.

It is hard to say exactly why underprivileged individuals being passed over for a promotion happens so often. Perhaps this is due to fulfilling a stereotype, for example, that ethnic minorities are hard workers but cannot make their voices heard.

Perhaps we are just simply not used to seeing ethnic minorities, disabled staff, or women as leaders, so deem them as not the 'right stuff', either consciously or unconsciously. Perhaps it is something else completely. Either way, it is a phenomenon which has a strong link to how we believe our staff can grow.

I recognise that promotions are complex. Few organisations have genuine transparency on how promotions occur. I also recognise that I have also met a lot of older BAME staff who have no visible ambition to move upwards either, or who therefore would not be the best person for the role.

Nevertheless, there may also be a phenomenon of individuals internalising their lack of opportunities as proof that they are not worthy of greater opportunities. If you were starved of stretching work for numerous years, you would probably lose interest after a while. I have met plenty of staff who have become disillusioned due to not being given the same opportunities as their peers.

I previously attended race workshops where BAME staff were given a safe space to openly talk about these issues. The first time I attended, I was shocked by how many disgruntled employees talked about the people around them were moving up, whereas their careers had been left to stagnate and wilt away. There was a large amount of resentment and anger within the room, and it was tough for the organisation to do much retroactively when the damage had already been done.

There was someone who was on a leadership talent programme. However, they explained that the promotion opportunities that white peers got were not provided to them. This was a consistent theme across different BAME staff across teams. It was incredibly hard to pass these things off as coincidences.

There was a view that younger, white staff were more likely to be promoted past them, particularly when they had a 'professional' look and a posher-sounding British accent. Looking at the organogram of the organisation and who was towards the top, it was incredibly difficult to argue that this was not the case.

I have also felt this personally too. I had a plethora of managers move above me making mistakes that would not be afforded to me. I ended up 'upwards managing them' to mitigate the mess my new managers were making. I went to a later iteration of a race workshop and realised that I was turning into one of those bitter members of staff. It was one of the big prompts that made me realise I needed to leave the organisation!

It is important to look at the development opportunities within the workplace, and whether these are truly equitable and available for people from all backgrounds. Whilst the criteria may be 'anyone may apply', in practice those who have strong mentoring connections, or friends in higher places that nudge to apply will be more likely to benefit.

Human behaviour and our ecosystem

Unfortunately, this tends to mean that those from disadvantaged backgrounds, be they BAME, women, disabled or another group, are far less likely to benefit from these opportunities. This goes back to the point around the difference between equality of opportunity compared to equity of outcome.

As an individual, take a moment to reflect on how you support others in their development. Perhaps you pride yourself on helping others and developing those that you come across – I know I do. For these groups, look at how fairly these opportunities are distributed. If you are white, and all your direct reports are also white, you may be inadvertently causing an imbalance.

Let me be clear here – I am not saying you should not support the people you encounter, even if they come from the same ethnic background or are of the same sex. However, this is an important point relating to the wider support of individuals from disadvantaged groups. You may want to think about ways in which you can support others outside of your normal circles. For example, certain organisations use BAME or women mentoring circles to help address this imbalance. This can help by giving a certain member of staff access they would not otherwise have held.

One quick note of caution: if you decided to mentor someone from a different, it is important to understand that their experience will be different to yours. I have certainly had my fair share of senior leaders mentoring me, all with the greatest of intentions. Some however failed to understand my perspective of some of the challenges I faced, instead giving me a list of tips for success that were not particularly helpful.

Specifically, I had senior leaders telling me that I just needed to be more assertive when being assertive with my points was getting me in trouble. As an ethnic minority, I was typically labelled as 'aggressive, whilst my white peers were seen as 'assertive'. They did not understand why this was the case, because as a white person this was not an issue they had ever faced before.

I have also had fantastic mentors who have understood that their journey is not directly applicable to me and have made efforts to understand the additional barriers I face which have not been the case during their careers.

A new trend is for 'reverse mentoring', essentially where senior leaders are paired with underprivileged individuals to learn more about the challenges they face. These have broadly been very enriching experiences for both involved and require zero cost to the organisation.

Coaching can also be excellent to explore these issues, as it takes away the necessity of having to learn from precise life experiences. Instead, it is more about learning from our own experiences and how we might take those lessons to support others. We will explore reverse mentoring further later in this book.

Halo and horns effect

Like in-group and out-groups, we often tend to gravitate to individuals that we prefer. This can often lead to us putting them on a pedestal, on which they are generally seen as competent. This is known as the 'halo effect'.

Likewise, there might be an individual who we do not like. We tend to complain about their work and see them as generally poor workers. This is the 'horns effect'.

The issue around halo and horns effect is that we tend to make character judgments which then lead to assumptions about their capability at work. For example, I have seen many young male workers impressing people around them through their confidence in speaking and through their sense of assertiveness in meetings.

These individuals may not necessarily be particularly good at their jobs, but they are still seen positively. If we fast forward and look later down the career line, we see that they are often promoted faster and thrown into new projects. Despite a track record of not being all that good at their jobs, they are seen as being 'made of the right stuff'. If you've ever been led by a leader who does not seem to have any idea what they ae doing, they probably fall into this category.

Meanwhile, those who are seen as 'bad eggs', are often treated as such. I have supported individuals who are new to their jobs and have gotten off to a bad start. Often this is not a fault of their own, but due to bad management. The result is that they have underachieved in a task or have had suboptimal outcomes.

This leads to questions about their competence, and can lead to 'performance improvement plans'. If you're not familiar with them, essentially this is a plan that does everything except improve performance. It deeply analyses all the flaws of the employee leaving them feeling unsupported, insecure, and questioning their self-confidence.

Unsurprisingly, most performance improvement plans lead to a termination of a contract. I remember being sorely disappointed in how this took place to someone I knew. The manager openly would ask how this individual got through university due to them having ADHD. In such an environment, it is nearly impossible to flourish.

From the eyes of this manager, whatever this individual did was negative. The decision had already been made that they were not capable, with HR unwilling to do anything to protect the individual. Despite the manager being known as particularly poor, no one from senior management was willing to step in.

I have experienced a horns effect personally. I had a first performance meeting two months into the role. I was told that all the work I had done was poor and substandard. I was also criticised for my 'demeanour', which showed I was disinterested in the work. I was shocked at the lack of feedback up to that point but quickly realised that my contract would be terminated if I did not improve.

Despite doing extra hours and proving I had done everything asked for to address the issues made, I was still terminated. On parting, my manager explicitly stated that I did not have what it takes to have a career in government. Five years later, I resigned from a different post in government, and only now, I was two promotions above the manager who gave me that assessment.

I am also wary of having the 'halo' effect around me. I ran our race and faith network with a large amount of success. Although many were still happy to give their opinions about what more needed to be done, I started noticing that individuals started to put me on a pedestal, meaning they inherently agreed with what I thought.

Of course, I am not an infallible human being, and I have no will of having my fan club! This was one of the reasons why I decided to step down after two years of leading the network, as I felt it would benefit from a change in leadership so that it was not too closely associated with me as an individual. It also did my ego good to have a break from being the leader!

In all, halo and horns effects reflect our human tendency to create heroes and villains. The protagonist is an infallible moral leader, whilst the villain is an evil, wicked individual. The reality of humans is much more nuanced, as such we would benefit from giving as fair an assessment to different individuals as possible.

In the space of diversity, this may mean that an individual who is terrific at their job may be problematic when it comes to how they treat their staff. Likewise, an ineffective member of staff may just be placed incorrectly within the organisation. To truly follow the principles of being inclusive, we need to guard against judging individuals with our preconceived notions. Instead, we need to judge people by the situation.

III. Understanding the current situation: diversity in the workplace

We have explored numerous different psychological phenomena that occur when we explore the issue of diversity. This plays a key role in the world of work. With our jobs being a significant period of our waking lives, they can play a giant part in people's wellbeing.

This is also critical to examine when we note the power a workplace can have on people. A better-paid job leads to greater affluence and an avenue to make a real impact in the world. For some, it is also about having a nice place to work with people you like.

Employee Surveys demonstrate that the experience of minorities tends to be worse than those of majority groups in the workplace. We also tend to see less representation at higher levels. It is important to examine why this is happening, and how this might be felt by those minority groups.

What are the common pitfalls?

I have had my eyes very sharply opened to some starkly negative experiences in the workplace. I will openly admit that this has been an uncomfortable journey. It can often be harrowing hearing the bleak experiences of those who have suffered.

Many of the issues we face stem from dysfunctional relationships and practices when dealing with one another as human beings. Sometimes these are intentional, but in workplaces often time these are behavioural patterns which we fall into.

For example, we may feel uncomfortable raising issues on odd leadership behaviours or do not feel it appropriate to share how we are feeling about certain decisions from our bosses.

Exploring this subject has also made me look far more deeply into myself. This was often quite uncomfortable for me too. At first, it was quite easy to complain about inequalities as I could tag myself as less privileged. I could tell others that they needed to understand the advantages that they had in their life, without ever stopping to consider that I might need to do the same process for myself.

I also have my life privileges. I went to a fee-paying school and had the benefit of attending university and studying abroad twice. I had great opportunities of growing up and living in the UK, with the expectation of a career and life fulfilment ahead of me. There were certain things that I found difficult, but this is nothing compared to most of the population in the world who do not have some of the most basic necessities: food to eat or a roof over their head.

This self-examination has been a humbling experience for me, and I expect it will be for you as well. Trying to genuinely get to grips with this subject will require far more humility, openness, and introspection than many other subjects you may have dealt with. The reward is becoming a better, more loving person. I would say it is worth the effort.

A key pitfall is not being able to sit with this sense of discomfort. The subject of diversity often brings up a sense of defensiveness, as it can often feel like an

68

attack on us as people. For example, people might get defensive at what can be what feels like sweeping statements being made about them and their background.

A common response is a denial of the existence of the problem or setting a set of 'what about' questions. For example, in the UK there is an issue of white working-class people being left behind. This is a real issue, however, when having a conversation about race, bringing this issue up only detracts from the conversation being held at the time. Rather than being helpful to white working-class people, instead just points out another problem and prevents a helpful conversation in a separate area.

My usual invitation is that there is certainly a space to talk about white working-class people, and if this is something that anyone is particularly passionate about, I would strongly encourage them to take up the cause and champion it. Honestly, quite often this does not lead to much uptake from people. It leads me to believe that the 'what about'-isms are often as much just to avoid the conversation as much as a genuine call to action on another issue.

Another challenging view is that this is simply not worth the time and effort – after all, why does it matter what we look like or where we come from if we get the job done?

I hope that my reflections may shed some light on that matter. The reality is that our background matters far more than we ever give it credit for. It shapes our values and beliefs about the world. It is also vital to better understand ourselves as humans. As a coach, I believe that understanding ourselves better is critical to leading a happy and fulfilled life, as well as having a better ability to serve others through what we do.

Another pitfall is the paralysis caused by not knowing how to raise the issue in the first place. One of the biggest problems in liberal institutions filled with well-meaning individuals is that they avoid the question completely as they feel it would be rude to ask about it.

In practice, this means a white manager being able to have a nice free-flowing conversation with their white report about their family and schooling traditions. When having the same conversation with a BAME report, the white manager avoids conversation for fear or being seen to be prying or saying something inappropriate.

From the BAME report's perspective, they find themselves having a less developed relationship with their manager and notice how much more sociable their manager is with their white colleague, compared to them. They subsequently feel excluded.

I give you permission to get this wrong. You will only learn by making mistakes. So, try and discuss this subject, and if you get it wrong, asked to be corrected.

From my experience, people are far more likely to be open to a discussion on their background based on the intention of the question and the way it is posed. If you ask in a genuinely inquisitive, curious way, you are likely to have a positive response. If you put someone on the spot to explain the views of their whole demographic in the middle of a meeting, this is less likely to work out well.

Why you may not have heard about these issues before

Sometimes it can be hard to understand what these diversity issues look like when we do not see them. So, let us use a working example.

A woman may bring up an issue about feeling treated unfavourably in the workplace by another male colleague, for example not being invited to workplace drinks, not being copied into emails, or generally not being addressed in meetings with respect. The women may follow standard procedure and bring this to the attention of their manager, who in this case is male.

The manager finds this surprising, and due to a lack of wider understanding around diversity issues can only process this issue in one of two ways. In his eyes, either this is a clear-cut case of sexual harassment (and therefore a serious HR issue they need to deal with), or this is a misunderstanding of the woman he manages.

Offices tend to be quite small, tight-knit and often cliquey cultures. The likelihood is that this manager already knows the accused male in question. From what he can see, the accused male is a nice, upstanding person, so what his female report is telling him does not correlate with his own experience. The male manager has also not seen any lewd or outright poor behaviour from the accused person towards women.

This, therefore, leads him to conclude that he is not a sexist. This leads him to rule out the first option. The response that the male manager therefore inevitably gives is that the woman must be mistaken, as the accused person is a nice guy and has worked here a long time without complaints.

Unfortunately, the male manager is not aware that his experiences are very different compared to the female he manages. He, therefore, does not think to question whether his experiences would be a good reference point for this situation.

He is also unlikely to hear about any individual issues against this person publicly either. Indeed, even if several female colleagues have made complaints, these would be in their own one-to-one chats. No one will ever piece these together, as they are all held in separate, private conversations.

The issue then is put back onto the female as her fault as she misunderstands, which inevitably makes her doubt her instincts. This makes it difficult for her to feel confident in her job when she is told that what she is feeling is imaginary.

If she is savvy, she may speak to other female colleagues and get a better idea of this male colleague's behaviour, and how to handle it. Whilst this helps, it does not solve the problem itself, and these other females will also probably tell tales that they've raised issues but been brushed aside.

From the female's perspective, at this point, it is better to give up on the formal system as the one-to-one conversations are ineffective. Whilst she could raise it more formally via a grievance, she realises this will likely result in a lot of discomfort, ranging from straining her relationship with her manager to retribution from the accused male. She also realises that she is unlikely to be believed in her claims unless she can bring definitive proof that it happened.

Thus, we find the full cycle of diversity issues not being addressed properly. It is worth pointing out that in this example, it is a man as both the manager and perpetrator, both of which are statistically more likely to be more senior in the organisation, whilst the woman may be in the minority.

This is only exacerbated with other diverse characteristics, for example, BAME individuals may not have other BAME people in the office to confide with to verify their experiences, simply due to a statistically lower amount in the population and therefore in the workplace. Not to mention if the woman in question was from an ethnic minority background.

Getting past the echo-chambers

You may be sympathetic to these causes, but ultimately not be sure what you can do. After all, are you best placed to deal with disability or race issues when you have had so little life experience dealing with them so far?

From the perspective of those who are passionate about diversity-related causes, it can often be difficult to engage people who are not from that demographic. For example, race issues are often talked about between ethnic minorities, women's issues between women, disability issues between disabled individuals and so on. What this creates are echo chambers. Whilst everyone inside these chambers agrees with the importance of the issues, few outside of these groups hear these messages.

This 'echo-chamber' dynamic happens because we feel that those who have a particular interest in those topics are best placed to deal with them. Unfortunately, what this means in practice is that little real action can take place. A wider dialogue needs to take place in terms of how we create our structures and how we treat those from different backgrounds by all people.

To take the example of women, many organisations both in business and civil society have perennial issues relating to equality of opportunity for women. And whilst any direct discriminatory laws (e.g., 'forbidding' women to apply for certain roles) are now illegal in many countries, there are still societal issues at play which stop women from climbing the ranks of an organisation in the same way a man would.

From an organisational level, women may find it hard to return to the workplace after leaving for maternity leave, and implicitly many organisations have an issue assuming that once a woman has started a family, their career will no longer be their primary concern.

Moreover, from a societal perspective, women are also expected to be the main caretakers at home, meaning they are often more likely to request flexible hours and time for childcare compared to their male counterparts.

Understanding the current situation: diversity in the workplace

If women are the only ones being engaged on this issue which is inhibiting women to make it to the top of the organisation, half of the population is not aware. If men (who make up the majority of boards as C-Suite executives) are unaware of these issues or avoid them as they feel it is not their place, this issue never sees the light of day. This is not to mention the reality that many will simply refuse to believe there is an issue in the first place, making this a much tougher situation to address.

So, if you are a man, it is important that you understand women's issues. But equally, this argument could be made about every group – an understanding of LGBT+ issues is important for straight people to understand, and race issues are important for white people to understand too.

It can easily get quite overwhelming how much there is for us to learn. It also really does not help that the subject is rather emotive, and it can be quite easy to get wrong even with good intentions!

The good news is that we can do lots to educate ourselves. We are not expected to understand everything, but we can help ourselves by being openly curious about the experiences of others outside of our own group.

The secret is in continuously learning. Each day is an opportunity to learn something new or to speak with someone with a different perspective. We can learn a lot about people in a surprisingly short amount of time when we show up open and curious.

Why we need to go further than the 'business case' of diversity

The business case for diversity is critical for us to shift this whole agenda from a 'nice-to-have' to a necessity in our organisations. Previously, business discussions on diversity were often pushed to the wayside once the 'serious' subjects of business priorities and budgets took precedence.

There is a growing understanding that this is short-sighted. We can now see that diversity is a vital part of an organisation to consider if they wish to continue attracting a wide range of customers and employees into their organisation.

We now better understand that our organisations should be engaging in diversity to secure new streams of income. None of this has been illustrated more so than the new proliferation of diversity-related jobs springing up following Black Lives Matter.

Unfortunately, hiring a chief diversity officer, or building a team to deal with the 'diversity problem' is not enough; these roles in themselves do little to effectively shift the dial if everything else about the organisation stays the same. Often diversity officers are given no budget, no team or direct accountability to the CEO, effectively making their roles powerless.

Worse still, in the age of social media, consumers (and indeed employees) are faster than ever to call out behaviours that they see as superficial or naked profiteering. An example of this would be the trending conversation about 'pink washing' which took place during LGBT+ Pride months in the UK and USA.

From an organisational perspective putting an LGBT+ flag on branding or posting may be thought of as a good gesture towards demonstrating support for Pride. From an LGBT+ activist perspective, however, if the organisation has done nothing to date to genuinely support LGBT+ issues, and indeed actively ignored the plights of its LGBT+ employees, this move is interpreted as hypocritical and termed 'virtue signalling'.

After the end of pride month, the LGBT+ flag disappears, and no real genuine action happens that genuinely supports the movement. Meanwhile, the company's social media is awash with positive messaging about how great the company is for displaying leadership on the subject. It does not take long for an LGBT+ activist to openly tweet about this, and it only takes an ex-employee to agree before you have full-blown public relations.

The unfortunate part of this situation is that there may have been genuine believers in the LGBT+ movement within the organisation who thought what they were doing was helpful. Perhaps some people even stuck their necks out to get this onto the agenda in the first place.

The consequence has led to even more fear and aversion from within the company from touching the subject ever again. Maybe you have been burnt by something like this, and now are wary of touching the subject ever again.

But whether you like it or not, pride month will come again, and as highlighted from the business case, wider diversity issues are only going to become more important.

When organisations get this wrong

It does not take long to browse Twitter or other social media platforms to find examples of where organisations have gotten this wrong. Think of the Pepsi Advert of several years ago featuring Kendall Jenner, which theoretically was to show support to protest around Black Lives Matter in 2017.

In practice, it angered the public as it trivialised protests for the benefit of a company wanting to make money. It has since been taken down, but you can find it by searching about Kendall Jenner and Pepsi online.

Whilst we may not know exactly what happened, from my own reading it sounded like the advert probably had positive intentions. The head honchos that approved it probably believed it would distil a message of unity, peace and understanding, by demonstrating that people can come together through their product.

I believe that this was a misguided attempt at doing something positive to demonstrate a forward-looking approach to diversity. Unfortunately, if organisations are unable to understand the subject in a particularly critical way, it can often lead to looking extremely out of touch to an ever-more vocal public. The fact that lots of us can remember the polemic around this advert demonstrates the risk of getting this wrong.

So how did a global corporation with some of the smartest minds manage to make such a large blunder?

One place to look is the make-up of the board itself. We are unlikely to find any black individual anywhere near the senior management board, nor any individual with particular expertise on diversity. This leaves quite a large deficit in critical thinking before the ad went out.

So, a more diverse boardroom may have helped, perhaps. Even then, it would be a lot to ask for one black individual to speak for the black population and expect them to be the filter for all things 'black culture'. Whilst it may have increased the chance of this being stopped before it happened, experience suggests that might not have changed a whole lot either.

Understanding the current situation: diversity in the workplace

If you're the 'only' in the room, it is tough to actively disagree with a proposal when everyone else is fully supportive. With minorities already having a reputation for troublemaking, they may not feel particularly encouraged to speak up against a problem even if it is a glaringly bad one.

Many of us know the odd dynamics of large boardroom meetings. All the senior people gather in a fancy meeting room to talk about important things. If we are lucky, half of them have read the papers, or are not distracted by their emails.

Whilst not having previously engaged with many of the subjects, nor read the background, this executive board now needs to make decisions. After all, the senior executives are paid for their decision-making skills.

This fire-from-the-hip style of decision-making may work when the subjects being talked about are those that executives understand, however when it goes beyond their realms of expertise it can suddenly turn into a bunch of rather wild opinions.

You may think I am being harsh on boards. However, I have experienced this first-hand when presenting on diversity. Whilst the boards have a good grasp of going through regular business agenda topics, the discussion on diversity often turns into lots of wide-ranging and often completely subjective opinions based upon the individual's own opinions.

This is particularly problematic when the individuals on the board have tended to come from the same backgrounds, meaning an opportunity to actively engage on issues such as women turns into what they may have heard from their wives or seen from their employees, which is extremely different to the reality of living those experiences and can lead to very wrong conclusions. An obvious example would be executives saying that there is not a harassment problem against women at their employment, not realising that they would never hear about it if there was an issue.

So, what can we do to improve the situation? Whilst one way to fix this is to increase representation on the board, this presumes that those minorities will always be well-placed to speak on behalf of their whole demographic.

From my experience, the first ones to rise the ranks are those that have done their best to blend into the culture of the workplace, meaning their awareness or willingness to speak up about issues is non-existent. They are uncomfortable speaking about these issues and probably have not previously as this would have branded them a troublemaker and halted their progress.

One way to test ideas and policies is to better consult a wider range of staff. Many organisations now have staff networks or employee resource groups (explored later in this book), representing individuals from certain backgrounds and characteristics. These can be an excellent way of getting honest views and constructive feedback on the organisation, and when supported correctly can be an invaluable resource for driving positive organisational culture.

Some organisations use these groups to actively test their policies and products. For example, an advert such as this could have been tested with a race network to better understand views before publishing it.

Likewise, certain staff from disability groups in other organisations have created products and policies to better serve disabled customers. This would come from existing resources meaning products have been made practically for free by employees from different backgrounds.

Whilst staff networks can help, fundamentally, I believe the real solution is greater diversity-based intelligence within the boardroom in the first place. After all, a board is never going to ask its staff networks for comments on its products unless they first realise their limits.

If leaders can appreciate the importance of addressing diversity issues sensitively, this will lead to a much stronger approach. This will allow them to harness the positive aspects of diversity – both for their organisations as well as their customers.

How it plays out in the boardroom

Below is a fictionalised example of what can often happen in the workplace when discussing diversity. Whilst this example is not 'real', it reflects what can often happen when looking to address diversity through the corporate systems currently in place.

A meeting is called. The main executives and HR are invited in. The aim is to solve the diversity problem. The agenda item is scheduled for 20 minutes. At this meeting it has been put top of the agenda, as it had been scheduled in previous meetings but was put at the end so was never addressed due to the other agenda points overrunning. With a new diversity reporting deadline approaching, the board need to nail it down now.

The meeting was called due to a new government initiative wanting to promote more women in the boardroom. This caught the organisation by surprise and led to some thoughts about where exactly all the women are.

HR does not usually attend but is invited in. They have spent the last two weeks scrambling around to understand where the women are in the organisation. They have built an initial analysis.

The meeting begins. HR starts presenting that women are particularly prominent in certain areas such as her own area, but otherwise are overly represented at junior levels, predominantly with receptionists and customer service workers.

One executive butts in that this is not true for their department, as there is one woman on his leadership team who is very visible.

HR note this point and says that some women are making it to middle management but do not often progress further at a certain stage.

Another executive jumps in to share his experience that the women he has worked with have generally worked well and have always been happy. It does not make sense that there is an issue. He suggests that perhaps this is simply an issue of time needed for change to happen.

Understanding the current situation: diversity in the workplace

The chair jumps in to clarify why there seems to be a drop-off rate in the middle management ranks. HR suggests this is related to women going off on maternity leave.

Another executive jumps in on this point, expressing that the issue is that women do not seem to aspire to senior management, particularly when they have started families. He notes he was having a conversation with his receptionist on this exact point, and she stated that she was not interested in progressing with her career.

The chair notes the point but is not convinced. He asks whether any of their competitors have the same issue. The room mumbles and generally agrees that they do, noting that the last time they recruited for high-level positions, women do not apply. They conclude that there must be a lack of suitably talented women for the role.

One woman is sitting in the room. She is deputising for her boss and is staying relatively silent. She is uncomfortable raising a point in front of a room that is more senior than her. The chair, noting a woman in the room, asks her what she thinks.

She fidgets in her chair, before talking a little about some of her experiences being one of the few women at her level. She did not have children, so did not face some of the challenges her other women colleagues did, who ended up leaving the organisation. However, she finds it difficult to explain this fully when being put on the spot. Her comments are politely noted by the rest of the board members.

The conversation continues, breaking down into a general set of opinions from different people, often with little coherence with one another. When it becomes obvious that time is running out, the chair pushes for a decision they can make.

One executive exasperatingly remarks that they cannot solve an issue if women do not want the jobs. Whilst the chair sympathises, he highlights that they must be seen to act to meet the expectation of promoting gender equality.

As such, the chair pushes the board to decide that they commission HR to find a solution to the issue and will revisit the conversation in the New Year. The chair ends by highlighting his personal belief that gender equality is extremely important and a priority of the organisation. He then moves to the next agenda topic.

***

This tale is a fictitious account but unfortunately is not particularly far away from what tends to happen. Diversity is such a large topic that looking to discuss it in an executive meeting rarely functions well, due to the innate lack of understanding.

When discussing most subjects, we usually want some level of subject matter expertise from the people in the room. Unfortunately, when it comes to diversity, the structures are not in place.

Whilst boards may be starting to recognise this, what then happens is they invite their diverse individuals to come in and present the issues and solutions. Whilst this is a noble intention, this often ends up inviting one vocal person who has strong views on the topic, rather than a more professional and evidence-based view.

Organisations are now employing specific diversity and inclusion professionals for this very reason; however, they are still often severely under-resourced and overburdened with 'fixing' the problem for the whole organisation.

As we see this play out in practice, diversity leads can be ineffectual if boards see hiring individuals as the solution in itself. This often means that the responsibility of the agenda is farmed out from leaders to this single D&I professional. They are unlikely to be able to do much on their own, as any substantive change will need to be backed from the top of the organisation.

The failure of organisations to tackle racism

When former Yorkshire Cricket Club (YCCC) player Azeem Rafiq made allegations about racism during his time at the club which led him 'close to committing suicide',[17] one of the first interventions came from Roger Pugh, then Yorkshire South Premier League Chairman. Pugh took the uninvited opportunity to highlight Rafiq as 'discourteous, disrespectful and very difficult'.[18]

'Indeed, over the five years in which we have been in existence, he is the only person in our league that I had any issues with... I am not a religious man, but a biblical quote seems to me apt here. It is, "as ye sow, so shall ye reap."'[19]

In other words, Pugh took the opportunity to say that Rafiq deserved to be subject to racist abuse due to him being 'difficult'. Pugh was later forced to resign but offered no apology when doing so.

This event in itself would be quite shocking. Unfortunately, the saga around the Yorkshire Cricket Club's handling of racism has only gotten worse from there. I have found this disappointing, both as an avid cricket fan and had previously gone to Headingley – Yorkshire's ground – several times as a student during my time in Sheffield.

With a high ethnic diaspora around Yorkshire, these actions demonstrate a club more worried about saving face than genuinely being interested in tackling racism, let alone building an inclusive relationship with minorities.

For anyone who has worked in diversity roles, the following sequence of the 'investigation' around these events is not particularly surprising (even if they can be depressing). Following the reports of racism, YCCC first ordered an 'independent' investigation. The 'independent' firm was Squire Patton Boggs, a

---

[17] https://www.espncricinfo.com/story/azeem-rafiq-was-on-brink-of-suicide-after-experiencing-racism-at-yorkshire-1231162

[18] https://www.espncricinfo.com/story/yorkshire-league-chairman-resigns-in-wake-of-azeem-rafiq-comments-1233619

[19] https://www.espncricinfo.com/story/yorkshire-south-premier-league-chairman-verbally-attacks-azeem-rafiq-after-racism-allegations-1231545

former employer of the Yorkshire board's chairman, Roger Hutton. The investigation was to be over the course by Xmas 2020.

Instead, it took until August 2021. On the Yorkshire board, itself were two of the accused members of the investigation – chief executive Mark Arthur and director Martyn Moxon. In other words, several of those implicated had decision-making authority on what happened with the report.

After this long delay, the Board issued 'profound apologies' after it found Rafiq was a 'victim of inappropriate behaviour', however they deemed there was insufficient evidence around evidence of institutional racism.

This was all done without the report being released (claiming they could not due to 'data privacy'), meaning a complete lack of transparency and questions only getting louder around the real contents of the report.

In September, the Board eventually released a summarised finding of the report which found that Rafiq was the victim of 'racial harassment' and 'bullying'. However, once again they reiterated that they could not release the report and that there was no evidence of institutional racism.

By October, political pressure started to mount. An Employment Judge ordered YCCC to give the full report to Rafiq by 8 October. A leaked version of the report highlighted that Rafiq was continuously referred to as P*ki – a slur against South Asians – by teammates. Whilst the original version was reported by media to suggest this did indeed show a culture of racism, the Yorkshire board disagreed, and overruled this judgement, instead describing it as 'banter'.

Other comments included teammates of Rafiq asking him whether his uncles owned corner shops and at one point a senior player approaching Rafiq and a few other South Asian players. This individual stated that there were 'too many of you lot, we need to do something about it.

YCCC doubled down and released a report stating they were 'pleased' to announce their actions – no player or coach was deemed to face disciplinary action. Later, another teammate, Gary Ballance came out and stated he was the one who used the racist slurs but did so in an environment where this was commonplace and said he was a close friend of Rafiq.

With the lack of movement and growing anger at the opacity, sponsors pulled out – Nike announced they would not renew their deal, whilst Emerald Group, Tetley's and Yorkshire Tea were ending their association. The England Cricket Board also suspended international matches at Headingley. Roger Hutton then resigned as the chairman of Yorkshire with immediate effect. Arthur and Moxon stayed until eventually being pushed out.

Rafiq along with the YCCC Board members was eventually summoned in front of the House of Commons Digital Culture, Media and Sport Committee, where Rafiq spoke of a toxic atmosphere within the dressing room in an emotional outpouring.

So, what can we learn from this sorry state of affairs? On the one hand, it is positive that politicians, sponsors, and fans are acting against what looked like a cover-up of the situation. On the other hand, this event highlights how ill-equipped a business such as Yorkshire Cricket Club is at dealing with a culture of racism within its organisation.

Moreover, it demonstrates how the interest of the organisation can shift to cover its back rather than deal with the issue at hand. It also highlights the difference between what an organisation says it does, compared to how it is in reality.

I saw a recent PR blast from YCCC around its pathways and inclusion activities to try and brush away the questions being asked. Internally, Arthur and Moxon sat on the Equality and Diversity Committee within YCCC, which demonstrated how flawed the internal setup towards diversity was.

These sorts of incidents occur in many organisations. However, many are not public-facing organisations like Yorkshire Cricket Club, meaning these attempts at obfuscation and faux-action often succeed. For Rafiq, he had to wait over a year since the investigation was launched, and any attempts at genuine accountability were resisted to the bitter end.

Organisations must not assume that they do not have racist or uninclusive cultures simply because they affirm 'they are not racist'. Allegations such as these need proper mechanisms to be dealt with, and these need to be taken seriously. With a growing level of consciousness around the issues of racism in the workplace, these sorts of cases are only going to become more common.

Understanding the current situation: diversity in the workplace

From a personal perspective, I believe this is going to be a long-term shift in organisational culture. That is not to mention what it means for me on a personal level (would I want to attend a Yorkshire Cricket Club match in the future?).

The original allegations also brought up stories of racism that members of my family faced at the grass-roots level which are still commonplace. I saw a relative of mine talking about a time when he came onto the pitch when he was asked if he spoke English, despite growing up and living in the UK all his life.

To me, this whole saga demonstrates the importance for organisations to continue working on diversity and inclusion and embedding it in their culture.

Organisational solutions which often fail

From an organisational perspective, diversity programmes often are unsuccessful for several reasons. Most predominantly, a lack of serious-buy in from senior leaders often undermines any chance they have. if the top does not genuinely believe that diversity is important, it is unlikely to have much traction.

Changing the representation of an organisation is much akin to a change management programme. Similar to a change management programme, it requires a large amount of buy-in due to the sheer amount of time and effort required to make it happen.

Without sufficient levels of support, diversity programmes will often get deprioritised when the next urgent action comes in, and often this can be seen in organisations where the response to any diversity issue is that 'now is not the time'. This is the answer that has been heard for decades, so it more sounds like the issue is being kicked into the long grass.

Organisations also fail to take diversity seriously in terms of dedicating genuine resources and effort towards them. Once senior leaders understand that this is an important issue, the solution then becomes creating a shiny strategy.

Unfortunately, without any actual resources going behind the creation of the strategy. It can be quite amazing to see organisations which are otherwise meticulous in the execution of their work being so floaty about aspirations on diversity. These strategies can often have no realistic measurement or execution plan.

Additionally, when a strategy is launched, little is done to include the voices of a wider group within its creation. Middle managers, who have not had the amount of training on diversity simply see this as another corporate ask. This means they often ignore it, or worse, actively resent another 'message from the top'.

So, it is important that people are taken on the journey about why diversity is important, and why change is needed. It is not enough for the Executive Board to understand it and issue edicts. I remarked on how well organisations are built to execute leadership decisions in wider business areas. However, when it came to actions around diversity, the lack of accountability meant that little happened. As the message cascaded down the organisation, no one was responsible for it. Whilst managers were meant to do something, it often fell down the priority list with all the other pressing issues they were dealing with.

Diversity and inclusion also suffer from the plight of bringing in whoever is interested or passionate about the subject, without necessarily giving adequate training or professionalisation. This often takes the form of inviting one BAME person or woman in a team to explain the plight of their people.

This can be very uncomfortable for the individual. It also can lead to building a whole strategy based upon essentially one vocal person's opinion, which will never be genuinely representative or get the buy-in it needs.

Genuine experience and expertise are important. This is the case as it would be in pretty much any other business area. As diversity conversations often evoke emotions, it takes skill to manage such conversations.

I am regularly in meetings where opinions fly around about what the most important issue is or why we need to create some brand-new scheme that is doing the latest rounds. These need to be managed and funnelled into effective action. Otherwise, there are few tangible outcomes to these discussions.

Gaining ideas from a broad range of people is a critical part of what diversity is about. However, that does not mean that a professionalised approach is not necessary. Building expertise within your organisation and empowering individuals to deliver a programme will bring far greater success. This is in contrast to the hodgepodge of ideas that come out in a 60-minute senior leader meeting to 'solve' the problem.

There is more to do to give diversity a clearer status within an organisation. Too often this space is covered by volunteers, or as part of an all-encompassing HR role, rather than a particular area to work upon in of itself.

Working in the space of diversity and inclusion within an organisation can often be lonely. You might be one of the few working on it. The importance of the issue is often disputed by seniors, and you are given few resources to 'solve' diversity for hundreds if not thousands of people. It can be hard to know what whether you are doing is effective.

Organisations would benefit from recognising these challenges better and doing more to support staff working on diversity. Naturally, we do not live in a world of unlimited budgets, but quite often simple, non-cost-based tasks like better valuing the work of these individuals will greatly increase the effect that can be made.

The move towards more inclusive leaders

In more recent times, organisations have looked at improving the inclusive leadership skills of their executives. This goes some way in dealing with the deficits in this area.

Deloitte has built out a framework to view the key signature traits of an inclusive leader, highlighting six different areas. These are commitment, courage, cognizance of bias, curiosity, cultural intelligence, and collaboration. Their report entitled 'The six signature traits of inclusive leadership' sets this out in detail.[20]

Commitment highlights the importance of continued action within this area. The research also notes that whilst extrinsic motivators (i.e., pay rewards) are relevant, the primary motivator was usually intrinsic motivators based upon an individual's values of fairness and equality.

Courage is a signature trait as inclusion often requires speaking up to challenge others and the status quo. Genuinely addressing diversity and inclusion often means challenging the way things have previously been done. It puts the individual under the spotlight and risks them being penalised for questioning authority. It is also about being courageous enough to speak about themselves in a personal way on their limitations.

Cognizance of bias is about having a high level of self-awareness, which they then act upon. These individuals understand the issues of unconscious bias and look to actively counteract these problems, both within the organisation as well as for themselves.

Curiosity is key for a leader to want to continue learning more about the subject. This is linked with open-mindedness, inquiry, and empathy. The idea moreover is to actively seek people who will have divergent opinions and withhold their judgements that might stifle the flow of ideas.

---

[20] https://www2.deloitte.com/us/en/insights/topics/talent/six-signature-traits-of-inclusive-leadership.html

Culturally intelligent leadership is understanding cultural similarities and differences, whilst also having an understanding that the leader's worldview is impacted by their own culture. These individuals also actively look to learn more about different cultures and build stronger connections with them. These leaders are also more tolerant of ambiguity and understand the importance of being authentic whilst not 'going native' in a new cultural environment.

Collaboration is about individuals working together. In this context, it particularly talks about bringing together diverse individuals. These leaders encourage autonomy and empower their team to connect with others. They also highly value the diversity of thinking and are wary of biases that might bring a group towards a status quo.

The report goes on to suggest actions, namely, making these traits a core part of a diversity and inclusion strategy. This should also be linked with a wider organisational narrative and expected behavioural statements. These traits should also be part of the recruitment process and brought into capability management models and performance management systems.

Organisations should actively reward individuals for exhibiting these traits, and build leadership development plans for individuals based upon them as well. Finally, this can be also integrated with things like wider innovation strategies and other processes.

Overall, this is a far more holistic way of integrating diversity. It is looking at building it into the wider processes an organisation has, rather than creating a strategy in a silo.

The Deloitte framework helps us understand what 'good' looks like in the space of being an inclusive leader. It sets some level of benchmark of what it looks like when people do this well.

Nonetheless, it is one thing to know what 'good' is, it is another thing for this to be achieved. Some organisations pay little due regard to inclusive leadership, and for those organisations that do see it as important, not much changes in practice.

Understanding the current situation: diversity in the workplace

As with a large number of diversity initiatives, these often get overlooked when a more urgent action comes along. In the context of inclusive leadership, this can often happen when financial short-term goals are prioritised, meaning that poor inclusive practices of leaders are overlooked due to the general performance of the individual.

Similarly, rushed hiring or favouritism can lead to any aspirations of an inclusive leadership culture being undermined. An inclusive leader is also hard to measure, and reports of someone not being inclusive are unlikely to arrive in the inbox of those one level up in the management chain; a more junior employee is unlikely to speak up against a poor or unfair boss.

Later on in this book, we will look at how you can better embody being a diversity champion. But first, let us take some time to understand what diversity means to you.

IV.   What diversity means to you

With the sudden outpouring of energy and emotion around diversity issues, it can feel pretty overwhelming to know how to react.

The interest in diversity has not appeared overnight. Like any event that shocks a nation (and subsequently the wider world), the killing of George Floyd sparked an outrage of feelings that had been hiding under the surface for decades.

You may have seen incidents in the news before the events of Black Lives Matter, or perhaps a notable headline or two. Nevertheless, these never conveyed the amount of feeling and emotion held by people.

The next chapter of the book will look at what diversity means to you. Whether you are someone who has cared about the issue for a long time, or someone who has only recently taken an interest in learning more, this will help you understand your own views better.

If you are someone who has cared about diversity for a long time, it can be helpful to return to the root reasons why it has mattered to you. We sometimes forget that there is a reason that this matters to us, but remembering this is a critical part of remembering why we want to do something in the first place.

If diversity is something newer for you, we will look at some of the reasons why issues around race, gender or other diverse groups may have not been apparent to you previously. For example, this could be to do with where your friendship groups lie. It could also be your source of information.

If you are feeling either sceptical or cautious about what I am saying, I invite you to keep an open mind. My aim here is not to tell you off, nor to not change the past. Instead, it is to build greater awareness and understanding that we can bring into our present actions.

Finding a starting point

From earlier chapters in this book, we have seen that Diversity is important. We recognise that it is also important to understand the issues of different groups we are not a part of.

The challenge is that there is a lot of information out there. You may have friends from certain groups that have strong opinions about certain subjects. You may have also realised that you know other people from the same group who might vehemently disagree with that very position.

For example, you may have grown up to have been told that calling someone 'black' is highly offensive, and meanwhile, you see more and more people themselves calling and identifying themselves as black. They may find it odd that you find it uncomfortable to do so.

I once recall being at school in a predominantly white environment. I was a member of a chess club and was asked who I had last played against. I replied that it was someone who I could not remember the name of, but they were black. Everyone around me stood in shock horror as I dared to use that word, following which they were confused as to whether I could be racist as someone with a South-Asian background.

The whole experience was pretty jarring. Looking back on it, I doubt that individual would have particularly cared about being called black, and I do think my white friends were being especially jumpy.

Unfortunately, there is no simple answer to many of these issues. It can sometimes be like poking our head above the parapet and finding a war raging on filled with emotion about identity and experiences. So it's understandable to feel out of place when we venture into these conversations.

These discussions are uncomfortable, and in some respects, they are meant to be. The point of these discussions is ultimately to shift our own understanding by listening to different opinions.

It may relieve you to know that you do not need to become an expert on this overnight. Like any skill you have learnt in your life, it takes time to build an understanding, in the same way you learnt to read and write, form political opinions, or build business acumen. It's never too late to start. So, whilst it may feel daunting, it is easier to see this as a journey of continuous learning. We learn a little each day.

After all, it is impossible to know everything about every single facet of human diversity. You could spend a lifetime trying to understand everything there is to know about all the different groups and their experiences, only to find that a new generation has grown up with their own new set of thoughts and opinions.

So, let's find a starting point, and what better place to start than looking at it from the point of view of you as an individual?

What diversity means to you

CUBE model

To help you better understand your own opinion on Diversity I will be introducing to you the 'CUBE' Model. This is a framework I created to help you think about the different areas of your own life and how they have been affected by the circumstances of your life.

'CUBE' spells out:

Culture

Upbringing

Bias

(Lived) **E**xperience

The model serves as a prompt for you to better understand yourself.

The question of how your culture or upbringing has shaped you may not have crossed your mind, apart from perhaps when you have travelled abroad and noted how different people do things elsewhere.

You can work through this model yourself individually or by sharing it with a partner. I have used this model in workshops which have resulted in very rich conversations. You can find an online handout of this model by heading to my website https://tahmidchowdhury.co.uk/resources/

You can also use it to look at life through the lens of someone who you know well but who comes from a different background You will likely get some way through to thinking about their life in a way you have not before. You will also probably find that there are gaps that you will simply not know about.

This can be an excellent prompt to having that conversation and building that understanding for yourself. Moreover, by doing this exercise, it can be a great

96

way to have a conversation that you may have felt uncomfortable to do so otherwise.

Some organisations have introduced 'reverse mentoring' (which we explore later in the book). This is where a more junior member of staff coming from a diverse background mentors someone more senior themselves. The idea of this is so that the junior staff can give their own perspectives on their experiences both inside and outside the organisation.

I have reverse mentored myself, and both I and my 'mentee' found it a valuable experience. She gained a lot from me explaining more about my own culture and upbringing, whilst I also learnt a lot from spending time with a senior and understanding more about their journey, as well as the pressures they face in their role.

Using the CUBE model is extremely well-suited to reverse mentoring. You can both go through the question prompts in this exercise and come back to discuss them with each other. It is a great way to frame reverse mentoring for an enlightening discussion.

Why bother with a 'model'?

The model aims to give you prompts to think about certain aspects of your life that you may not have done so before.

It will not instantly 'solve' any issues or fix your organisation's diversity problem, but it will help you start the journey of understanding more about diversity, and what it means for you. As mentioned earlier, building your own understanding of your views of diversity is critical for you if you want to genuinely care about it.

the point of this is to get you thinking. You may find parts of the model that you like more than others. You might choose to frame certain questions in a different way than I have. That is fine.

What you will likely find is that this will prompt you to think about something you probably have spent a lot of time thinking about already, but also reveal something you had not.

You will also probably find that if you were to revisit it in six months or a year, it will likely be quite different to how you respond to it now. This demonstrates the shifting perspectives we have as humans as we continue to develop.

Culture

Culture can be defined in many ways. Here, we mean the culture that you experienced when you were growing up. In particular, the things that explicitly influenced you (e.g., music influences, shift in generational culture as you were growing up) but also the more implicit things.

For example, what was the general expectation in society for you when growing up? Were you expected to grow up and get married? If you were the male, were you expected to be the breadwinner to pay the bills? If you were a woman, was it to take care of the children?

The aim of examining culture is to better understand what particularly affected you from a societal perspective when growing up.

I experienced a mix of cultures as a second-generation British-Bangladeshi. I had both the cultural influences of the UK where I spent the majority of my life and where I went to attend University, but I also was impacted by Bangladeshi culture – close knit-families and traditional structures.

I also experienced a very different way of how society was structured when living in Bangladesh for two years in my youth, such as a stricter style of schooling, the regularity of domestic servants in households, the large-style celebrations of public holidays and the rich mixture of different foods and cuisines.

On top of this, as a second-generation migrant, I have had a different experience from my parents. There is a tension I felt of not belonging in either 'culture' as I am not quite British enough to be British, nor am I Bangladeshi enough to be Bangladeshi (e.g., my Bengali fluency is poor, and the way I think, act and speak betray my western upbringing). This particular mix of cultures has therefore had a profound impact on my view of life.

So, bringing this back to you, how has your culture affected you? You do not need to have an overly elaborate answer like mine but thinking about this question might be the first time you have done so in a deeper way. The point of this is not to have the most whacky and wonderful tale, but rather to identify that culture *has* had an effect on you, and the likelihood is that the way you feel is very different to others – whether they be from the same culture or a different one.

Questions to consider:

What is your culture?

How has your culture defined you?

How important is your culture to you?

How do you feel about other cultures?

Upbringing

Upbringing examines your unique experience of growing up. This is probably one of the more straightforward sets of questions, as it essentially looks at how you were raised, and how much that affected you in terms of your ambitions and goals, but also your character and values.

You may have come across the idea that much of what forms us stems from our upbringing. From a diversity perspective, it helps explain why we think how we do, and why we may act in a certain way which is very different to someone with the same background.

Think about the values that were instilled into you, either implicitly, or explicitly by your parents and wider family. For some, this may be based upon religious messaging based upon your parent's faith, but it is also likely shaped by their own experiences.

For example, was there an implicit understanding you should follow your father's footsteps into the societal trade? Did your parents have a difficult time financially, so emphasised the importance of finding a good job to ease your future burdens?

The questions could go on infinitely; ultimately, you will know your upbringing best. So, try and examine how this has formed you as a person and how much this has shaped your thinking. From a diversity perspective, understanding how much this has shaped your personal view of the world can go a long way in understanding the importance of family and upbringing for others.

For example, many BAME individuals are often told that they will need to work twice as hard as their white counterparts, and as such, there is this pressurised mentality that they internalise. This can manifest itself in individuals with a particularly keen work ethic, but also lead to an inferiority complex, and higher rates of imposter syndrome.

If you are a manager, understanding these perspectives can be invaluable for motivating your employees. Even if you are not a manager, being a friend or colleague who understands these issues will deepen your relationship and build

What diversity means to you

your emotional intelligence when dealing with others.

For me, my upbringing was particularly pronounced in the expectation of me to be religious, follow my family traditions (e.g., arranged marriage) and follow wider expectations upon me in terms of areas such as excelling in school and grades. I reflect that the intended effect was quite different to the actual effect it had on me - it pushed me more towards a rebellious mindset when I was younger.

Questions to consider:

How were you brought up?

How has this framed your beliefs?

How might this be similar/ different to others?

Bias

When we talk about bias, we are talking about the preference for or against something. In this context, we are examining how people in their nature prefer interacting with certain groups.

Most often, this is a tendency to spend time with people who are like us, leading us to have a certain aversion – whether consciously or unconsciously – to having the same interactions with someone from a different group.

Bias can sound like a quite heavy or loaded term, but it is an important concept when relating to diversity. These invisible biases play a part in understanding why individuals from diversity groups can often feel excluded from groups, when from your perspective there may be no direct reason for them to not feel included.

It is the reason why BAME individuals and women can often feel far more excluded in the workplace, as they feel different and so are far less comfortable operating around others when they are in the minority group.

Everyone has biases to some level, and a lot of these come from our upbringing. Growing up in a South Asian household myself, I grew up with explicit negative views of black people coming from comments around me in my family.

Many years later, this shaped me to have negative assumptions about their abilities in the workplace, particularly those from older generations. This is something I had to actively identify and work on to overcome a bias in myself. Likewise, there were similar internalised views of women I held from my background.

Bringing this back to you, perhaps the easiest way to understand the concept of bias is to think of examples of when you were negatively affected by one. You may not have been in lots of cross-cultural dialogue where these issues were discussed, but you are likely to have found yourself in a situation with the opposite sex.

If you are a man, perhaps you have heard the opposite sex presume that you are unable to express yourself emotionally or presumed to react negatively by displaying violence or aggression. You may have also internalised the belief from growing up that you must be the breadwinner and that you must follow the family career. Perhaps you have had none of these experiences, but something else entirely.

If you are a woman, there are probably more obvious examples that you can call upon. These range from the idea about whether you can have a career whilst having a family, being expected to be feminine in actions or being asked to smile more, catcalling and harassment either in the street or in the workplace.

Take an example where people have made assumptions based upon whether you are a man or a woman that has made you uncomfortable. Take a moment to explore how this feels in more detail. You will probably find this experience may bring up quite negative emotions about how frustrating it is that others presume to know you without asking you.

In terms of diversity, many presumptions or stereotypes can have profound effects on individuals from these groups. These can have very negative impacts on their livelihoods and careers. Innocent and accidental stereotyping include throwaway remarks to women that they will not be interested in their careers after starting a family or greeting a black man as a security guard rather than the CEO (which has happened!).

It can be helpful to open a dialogue with someone from a different group who will most likely have a plethora of stories once you dig deep enough.

Some of the experiences I have shared from the workplace included getting a new job on promotion but not being introduced to the team. I then saw a new white colleague joining the next week and getting a full introduction.

Soon after starting the role, I met the head of my team who told me I would be okay because it was a discreet role. When I asked my white colleagues they never had anything like that - It was not the most motivating pep-talk I have ever had!

Questions to consider:

What does bias mean to you?

What negative stereotypes have you observed?

How might you have suffered any biases against you as an individual?

What biases might you have of others?

What diversity means to you

(Lived) Experience

The final part of the model looks at experience or lived experience. The idea behind this is to bring the other parts of the model – culture, upbringing, bias – together. Lived experience examines how these have played out in practice when looking at people's lives.

The key behind this is understanding the stories behind the different elements of diversity, and how it has affected us in the real world.

My family particularly emphasised academic achievement, a typical expectation within South Asian households. I was fortunate that my family were successful, as such I had a wealthy upbringing meaning I went to a fee-paying Methodist school. I had access to wider opportunities and extracurricular activities.

It also meant I went to a predominantly white, Christian school whilst being brought up in a Muslim, Bangladeshi household. Whether it was a mixture of being different or teenage angst, I grew up with a desperate desire to fit in. This was particularly felt when I saw people starting to go out and party, which I was simply not allowed to do.

Nonetheless, it did also allow me to go to university, including a year abroad in France and later a Master's in Belgium – here I gained a wider perspective of different cultures and for the first time genuinely questioned the idea of being seen as 'British' by continental Europeans who went on to ask me about the bland English food I would eat. I would have to explain to them that I would have curries as my meals for most of my upbringing.

Fast-forwarding to the start of my career, I entered the workplace with the expectation that work was broadly meritocratic. At the time, I thought of diversity as an odd corporate buzzword.

Quickly though, my assumptions of an egalitarian, meritocratic system were shattered when I saw how often workplace behaviours were dysfunctional, with the BAME staff often being left behind in junior positions.

106

What diversity means to you

My life was a complex mix of privileges and disadvantages. This has been a particularly useful exercise for me as it has allowed me to understand things better in terms of why I may have felt like an outsider, but also appreciate the privileges I had of a good education that many others were not afforded.

If I had not been in a school that pushed for academic excellence, I may have attained a far worse grade or perhaps not attended university at all. My life journey would have been very different

Lived experience is a particularly useful concept when discussing diversity. It allows us to look at the wider picture. Quite often we go into a workplace and look to initiate diversity schemes, but we often vastly underappreciate the experiences people have before we meet them to build up a wider picture of who they are. Looking through this lens also helps humanise the subject, which builds a better empathetic connection with one another.

As before, I invite you to look at this for yourself. If helpful, write your personal story on a notepad and examine what were the advantages and disadvantages you faced. Take a moment to think about how these have shaped your own life, and how it has developed to where you are now.

You can go as broad or as narrow as you want, though for you to make the most out of doing this, I suggest you give yourself a relatively rigorous examination. Watch out for assuming that certain things such as going to university or even having a stable household are the norm for everyone.

Questions to consider:

How has your background affected you to where you are today?

What differences might this have had compared to someone else from a different background?

has your background come up in your workplace/personal life? If so, how?

CUBE model questions

To recap, below is a non-exhaustive list to get you thinking more about each of the different elements mentioned within the model. The questions are very open-ended, and the point of this is to answer how you feel this best fits you.

I recommend you take a notepad and work through the questions at a pace that suits you. It is helpful to reflect on the question before answering, but equally do not agonise over the perfect answer either. If there are other questions that you want to explore, do feel free to do so.

If you are finding it difficult to ask some questions, try asking yourself how someone from a different background would answer this for you. (You can even ask someone you know well to do this for you to compare the results).

A fun exercise that I have used within a workplace setting is sending people off into small groups to ask each other these questions. It is highly effective and brings together a rich set of conversations that otherwise would not have happened.

Culture

What is your culture?

How has your culture defined you?

How important is your culture to you?

How do you feel about other cultures?

Upbringing

How were you brought up?

How has this framed your beliefs?

What diversity means to you

How might this be similar/ different to others?

Biases

What does bias mean to you?

What negative stereotypes have you observed?

How might you have suffered any biases against you as an individual?

What biases might you have of others?

(lived) experiences

How has your background affected you to where you are today?

What differences might this have had compared to someone else from a different background?

has your background come up in your workplace/personal life? If so, how?

V.   Embodying an active diversity champion

The last chapter looked at what diversity means to you, and how it relates to your personal experience. The next chapter is on how you can make a change in the way that you live your daily life.

Whilst understanding the nuances of the human experience is critical to understand how we are different, there is also a level of commonality in our lives as humans.

Many of the issues around diversity and inclusion stem from either poor communication or a lack of openness to a different perspective. Whilst tools such as the model we worked through in the last chapter are great to surface what these issues might be, the biggest change we can make is in the way we act in our daily life.

In this chapter, I will introduce to you concepts around the idea of the whole self and 'Being'. The idea of Being is based upon the question of who you are choosing to be in this moment.

At its core, it is asking the question of how you are acting as an individual, and how you are choosing to show up in the world. The implicit idea behind this is that we get to choose how we show up.

Who are you being, at this moment?

Are we in control of our feelings?

As humans, we can often feel like we are a victim of circumstance, and that our actions are based upon a response to the external world.

For example, let's take a day when we go to the shops. We pop in on the way to work. We see an interaction of a customer screaming as they are getting poor customer service. We are shocked by their behaviour and suddenly find ourselves being on edge for the rest of the day. We are frustrated at this other person for their poor behaviour. It bothers us for the rest of the day.

This experience leaves us feeling more on edge. When we're at work, someone asks us something whilst we're concentrating. This causes us to jump in surprise, which compounds our stress. From this space of stressed alertness, we receive an email request for something urgent. We feel an extra level of overwhelm. Why does this all have to be piling up on us today?

These moments spiral outwards into creating a day of stress and unhappiness for the people around us. We go home and spend time talking to our partner or housemates about the person at the shop in the morning screaming. We explain our indignation and how it set our day up to be a negative experience.

In our mind, we see that the source of our unhappiness was the alarming altercation in the morning. If we had not been witness to that act, then we would have had a much better day.

From this perspective, it's no wonder why many of us spend a large amount of time miserable – it's not exactly hard to find a negative story on the news about famine, deaths, and societal issues. Unfortunately for us, our brains are also more hard-wired to focus on negative issues than positive ones. It's our brain's way of keeping us safe.

Whilst our pre-historic brains were attuned to negative signals being a potential life or death situation, this is not well-adapted to our modern life, where we can easily fixate on all sorts of negativity to the point that we do not want to leave our houses.

However, there is another way for us to see the world. Rather than believing that our wellbeing is derived from the external world, we can choose to see it as coming from inside of us.

In practice, this means that we do not rely on the day going well to feel good about ourselves. We are happy with who we are. We are already content and fulfilled. This means we do not need anything from the outside to validate us, whether that be the recognition of others, a promotion or societal status.

From this mindset, something bad happening does not make much difference to our day. If we were to see the same situation of a person screaming in a shop, we could realise that this altercation does not need to fundamentally change how we feel. Yes, it might be uncomfortable at the time, but without the fixation on the outside world, we can go ahead and enjoy the rest of our day.

This mindset can be extremely powerful, as it can essentially shift our behaviour in most situations where we are put under pressure or have stressful deadlines. As we highlighted in earlier chapters, our propensity for quick, biased decisions is much higher when we are stressed. So, if we can find a way to let go of the pressures of the world, it can be quite literally life-changing.

The change I have seen in people who have shifted their mindset has been incredible. It has not only changed the way they lead teams and responds to people, but it also massively reduces their blind spots and any potentially damaging behaviours when they are stressed. From a place of calm, we are better, nicer human beings. It is what I focus on particularly when working with coaching clients.

Not only this, but I can also see that people who are more in control of how they think and feel are also far more effective. One senior leader I found inspirational during my time in government would always impress me with the way she would walk into a new meeting looking completely fresh.

Despite having been potentially chewed out by a minister for the preceding thirty minutes, she would come into a new conversation as if nothing had happened. This allowed her to be incredibly present without bringing the baggage of other meetings into her work. From this space, it was possible to focus on what we were all there for. It was no wonder that she was extremely well-liked, seen as highly competent and ended up getting picked up for an even higher post a couple of years later.

Shifting our relationship with thought

So, if changing the way we think about the world can have such profound impacts, how exactly can we do this? Well, the first thing is to look at our relationship with our own thoughts.

Many issues around diversity and inclusion can be based upon the idea that the view of the senior leader is the 'right' one, and that if they were in a situation where one thing happened, then that was the objective reality in their eyes.

I recall an instance where I noticed my head of team did not look me in the eyes when speaking to me. Instead, she would glance away when talking to me. It became a common pattern, to the point where I would notice that the way I was spoken to was different to the other people in my team. I even had a more junior member of the team come up to me, asking me if I knew that the way I was talked to was different to other team members.

Since I was new to the team, I decided not to create a fuss. However, when it came to performance review season, I decided to highlight that this was a cultural issue within the team. When I told my team leader that she had done this behaviour, she asserted that she did not. After all, she could not recall ever actively deciding to not look me in the eye.

To her, the objective reality was that she did not do this because she did not recall it ever happening.

Relying on one single person to know an objective reality is problematic for all sorts of reasons. For starters, many leaders do not recall many of the small things they do on a day-to-day basis, nor are they always present to see a situation. Even when they are present, they may not be looking at it from the same perspective as another person either.

Another instance was when I pointed out to my boss that I was interrupted by a more senior, white leader in the midst of providing my views in a feedback-giving exercise. My boss did not understand why this mattered as I was allowed to finish my point afterwards. However, from my perspective, an interruption by a senior white member of staff was rather off-putting, and it made me think twice about giving my opinion.

I do not know whether I was necessarily 'right', in my perspective. However, my perspective existed all the same. So, the view that one person can view the reality of the world is flawed as it takes away all the different things that can unfold at the same moment.

What we see as individuals is not objective reality. So then, what is it?

Our consciousness projects our realities onto a screen. In other words, we see what we want to see in the world. If we hold a hammer, we will look around to find nails to hammer in. If we think that all red ladders give us luck, we will spend a lot of focus looking out for red ladders.

By understanding that what we see in life is a projection rather than a reality, it becomes a lot easier for us to change how we see and react to the world. Rather than seeing news of a humanitarian crisis being the cause of our suffering, it is instead the negative thoughts we have about a humanitarian crisis which cause us to feel bad.

If we had never checked the news, we would have never known the humanitarian crisis even happened. So, the event in itself was not the cause of our suffering. And even if we do see the news, there is a reason some days it might not bother us, whereas on other days it does.

By shifting the relationship we have with our thoughts and feelings, we are suddenly far more in control of how we show up in the world.

So how does thought work?

An important part of understanding thought is that it is not something that we control. So, it is not to push ourselves just to think about happy thoughts.

I would say that feeling 'bad' is important. Feelings are what make life worth living. We cannot only feel 'good' emotions. 'Bad' emotions keep our lives in balance.

However, we get to choose whether we care about the things that are important to us or not. If something is not that important to us, we can let it go. And even if we are feeling bad about something we care about, we can understand that this is stemming from our thoughts rather than the situation itself. So, the more we think about how awful a situation is, the more we are causing ourselves to suffer.

From here, we can question whether our suffering is helping anyone. We often cause ourselves to suffer by spiralling in our thoughts. Byron Katie writes in 'Loving What Is' that we often try and fight with reality by wishing it was not so.

But wishing that something did not happen ultimately does not help anyone. It only causes us to feel worse about the situation. Not only this, but it also often leaves us feeling despondent or helpless. From this mindset, we are less likely to do anything to make things better. Whereas when we are calm and clear, we are in a much position to act.

One misunderstanding I hear is that it is the negative emotions that spur us on to react. I would invite you to look at how true that is. I remember having a conversation with someone recently about how the fact they were worried about their studies. They said that this was the reason that they ended up studying so hard.

When I asked them what they would have done if they were not worrying, they took a moment. In the end, they said they would have studied anyway because they wanted a good grade.

So, these negative emotions are not necessarily as productive as we think they are. We can do plenty to change the world without requiring negative emotions

116

to prompt us. When it comes to diversity, this is a key distinction. Many are driven to act because of negative feelings. Subsequently, we see high levels of burnout and mental health issues. There is another way – we can be more accepting of the reality of the situation and still act to change it.

That is not to say that the solution is to block out negative emotions in favour of positive ones. Toxic positivity can be unhealthy as it can push us to the idea that we are not allowed to feel sad or angry.

But feeling sad or angry are just natural emotions as part of the human experience. When we lose a loved one, it is part of the human experience to feel anguish. However, the thought-driven self-sabotage is when we start pondering the 'what-if'.

We can choose which thoughts we can focus upon. Thoughts are like a constant flow of information passing through our minds. We cannot stop them, just as we cannot stop our blood from circulating through our bodies. We have thousands of thoughts without us even realising them.

The reason our minds are not completely overloaded is that we do not focus on every single thought that we have. As I am writing this, I can see an empty coffee cup, someone writing notes by hand into a notebook and another person typing frantically into a laptop.

I can easily get caught up in thoughts about how I have not hand-written notes in a while. I can also wonder what the person on their laptop is writing about. As for the empty coffee cup – well it makes me think that I would like a fresh batch!

It's only when I have focussed upon these thoughts that they have started to shift my behaviour. Before looking to observe the coffee cup, I did not feel like having more coffee. But the thoughts of the taste of it have made me imagine how nice it would feel to have more. My mouth has started salivating, and I have started a new train of thought as to whether I have money to buy another. Perhaps this big description of coffee now makes you want to have a coffee too!

However, if I were to notice the coffee cup, but then go back to writing, it would not take me long to forget about the coffee. We only have thoughts for a few minutes. Despite writing about it a few paragraphs earlier, I had totally forgotten about the other people I had described earlier. It turns out those thoughts were not that important at all.

So, the thoughts that I have are not all that important in the grand scheme of things. This is not just the case for something as mundane as coffee or people, but also can be for pretty much anything. For example, imagine you are having a nice Sunday afternoon, perhaps enjoying a nice cup of coffee (clearly, I have spent too much time thinking about coffee in this chapter!).

You suddenly start thinking about how you have a lot of work to do on a Monday morning. Here, we have a choice. We often default to the choice of needing to think about it more. Suddenly, this Sunday afternoon becomes a lot less enjoyable, and we find ourselves stressing about the work we must do.

The thoughts are not helping us either as they only serve to make us feel more stressed. By the time Monday comes around, we are feeling more nervous about the day, rather than excited about what may come during the week.

We may decide that it is better to not think about the work. Unfortunately, what often happens is that we try and force ourselves to stop thinking about it. This does not work particularly well either, as the more we try and stop thinking about something, the more we end up thinking about it. Despite our efforts, the thought will happen anyway, and by giving it more attention, we have still made it control how we feel.

The way I have found it most effective is that we can simply let this train of thought roll through the station and let it pass. When we think of something like our work, we accept that it is something that has come into our thoughts and simply let it be. Without much effort or attention, the thought will simply pass by, like a leaf in the wind.

To illustrate this example in another way, I would invite you to **not** think of a big, pink flying elephant. Unsurprisingly, the first thing you will do is think of one. If you keep trying to tell yourself to not think about the elephant, the easier it becomes to visualise it.

So instead, let us just let our big pink elephant friend occupy some mental space now that we have thought about them. After a few paragraphs of reading, we'll find that the pink elephant is no longer in our consciousness.

When we can realise that our thoughts do not have to be as powerful as we make them to be, it frees up so much of our mental and emotional energy. From here, it is far easier to be the humans we want to be.

Who are you being?

By changing the relationship we have with thoughts, we can decide what things we want to focus on. So, if we want to be conscientious, inclusive leaders, we can decide to be one.

The emphasis on Being is a commitment that we embody on a day-to-day basis. The idea of Being is detailed in the book 'The Ultimate Coach', which describes the life of Steve Hardison.[21] He is a legendary figure in the coaching world and has coached world leaders and CEOs. His coaching agreements are often hundreds of thousands of dollars.

The idea of Being is the idea of what we are committing ourselves to be every day. We declare to ourselves who we want to be, which sounds simple enough but requires a level of dedication to ensure it becomes a reality.

To choose how we live our lives, we must first understand that the way we experience life is based upon how we decide to experience it.

For example, if we believe our day will be terrible as we need to go to the dentist, this will frame our day negatively. Yet if we see today as a blessing as it will allow us to ensure we are caring and treating our body, we can reframe the same situation in a completely different way.

The idea of Being may sound like a simple set of declarations which will magically change our world. But the reason it is so powerful is that we're committing ourselves to live by our ideals, and by doing this every day consistently, the magic will then happen.

If we are kind, caring and loving **every** day, in a year our lives would be completely different. If we committed to living and enjoying life **every** day, we would be extremely happy. The key is committing to it on a day-by-day basis and sticking to them. Sure, we can make a slip up here and there - we are humans after all, but we cannot expect change if we simply say that we are kind and caring but do not put this into practice in our day-to-day actions.

---

[21] Amy Hardison & Alan D. Thompson, *The Ultimate Coach* (2021)

The beauty of looking at this on a day-to-day basis is that it is much more practical. If I pass a beggar on the street, I can choose to be more charitable because I am intentionally doing so. If I were not to have committed to my being, it would be easier for me to simply ignore them.

I certainly do not give charity to every single beggar I meet, but I do give far more than I used to. This is because I am far more intentional about how I show up in the world. It has also made a large difference in the way that I am speaking with people. This includes servers in a restaurant and people that are more junior to me.

Since devoting myself to my own being, I have seen a profound shift in the relationships I have had in my life, and the way I see the world. I have deeper, more loving conversations with friends and family. In return, I find a greater sense of connection than I have ever done in my life. I feel a far greater sense of peace and fulfilment in life.

Whilst I would like to say that I was always 'nice' before, the reality was that quite often I would not have taken the time to ask how people were doing, because it did not seem that important.

Now it feels important as it is a goal I have set for myself. Even when I have not quite been as kind or caring as I want to be, I can recognise that I am human and look to reaffirm my commitments for the next day. That way, I do not have to beat myself up for not being perfect, or spiral into negativity.

Having your own 'document'

Steve Hardison sets out his commitment to Being – what he refers to as his 'document' – a series of statements that he reads every day to himself. The full document is extremely powerful, and as a daily commitment ensures that he acts with integrity with what he says about himself throughout his daily encounters.

I have decided against sharing Steve Hardison's document here out of respect for the process that goes behind understanding it. If you are curious, I would invite you to look into the book 'The Ultimate Coach'.[22] There you will find out more about his life, and how the idea of Being can make a grand shift for you.

Reading this book pushed me to write my document with the intentions that I want to embody daily. These are now placed in a frame in my office above my monitor as a reminder of what I commit myself to.

I would also invite you to hold off from any feelings that this might be boastful or coming from a place of ego. Nor are these about simply creating affirmations that will magically make us better people. Instead, it is about being ambitious in what we want to live into through these documents by having a clear vision of the being we want to embody each day.

Tahmid's Document

I am greatness, and I seek to create greatness around me.

I am change. I am the world.

I am kindness, support, and love.

I am driven by good and making good happen. I live by my beliefs and by my morals. Always.

---

[22] Amy Hardison & Alan D. Thompson, *The Ultimate Coach* (2021)

Embodying an active diversity champion

I am fulfilled, content and happy. I am my full range of emotions. Delight. Sadness. Anger. Laughter. I am all of these.

I am appreciated, supported, and loved.

I love people and honour and respect the different experiences of every individual on this earth.

I cherish my family, who support and love me in their own ways.

I cherish my ancestors, through whom I connect with the history of my people and a knowledge greater than my single being.

I am my experience, my knowledge, and my intellect. I am my thoughts and my persona. I am my body, how I treat myself and how I love myself. I am all these things and much more.

I am me. I am my actions, my commitments and dedication. I am my essence. I am my soul.

I am now. I am present. I neither regret the past nor long for the future.

I am no one, and I am everyone. I am connected to the spirit of the world. I connect with everything around me and the vibrations of the earth.

I am an omnipotent being who connects people and ideas to create incredible change.

I am an incredible force of nature that can achieve things beyond my wildest dreams.

I am beauty and love. I am extraordinary and unstoppable.

The name given to me is Tahmid.

How did it feel to read this?

For me, it gives me a sense of who I want to be. When I do not quite live up to my document, I can forgive myself and recommit to it. Living into the document is a daily practice.

In a corporate setting, it can be easy to state the importance of teamwork or being a caring person. Committing to act in this way daily takes an extra level of dedication, which brings us to act in a way that is far more intentional than we would otherwise. It means that we would act in the right way, no matter what we were feeling at the time, or even when nobody was watching.

If you would find it a helpful exercise, you could also look to write your own document. It is also helpful to review it regularly to see whether you are acting in integrity with who you are committing to being.

Embodying inclusive leadership

How does the idea of Being relate to diversity and inclusion?

Inclusion is based upon the fact that people are allowed to have different opinions and are allowed to share these within an organisation or team.

In practice, the degree to which an organisation is genuinely inclusive depends upon the context of how information is shared, and to what extent the hierarchical nature means one person is more 'right' than others.

To put it another way, the first step in embodying inclusive leadership is understanding that other people might have different points of view from you. This will mean that they approach things from a different perspective. You might go and ask other people for their opinions, from which you will form the basis of your opinions.

This is probably the level that many leaders are at. Whilst they do actively want to hear what their staff believe; they return to their own thoughts and judge what their version of reality is. Whilst this is better than not consulting at all, it still means that the 'real' version of the truth is based upon whatever the most senior person decides.

How this plays out in practice is often a disparate group of people giving different opinions. Following the consultation, the decision predominantly depends on how much the senior leader agrees with them.

The next level for leaders to embody inclusive leadership is to understand that they may sometimes be wrong, even if they are convinced that a solution is the right one. The human mind is incredible – it can create all sorts of realities. It can tell an incredibly convincing story about whatever decision we make. We've all had situations where we were convinced that something was correct, only to be bamboozled when we are proven wrong.

I remember working in a tourist spot, where we had a few work exchange students from France. One of the girls working there was convinced that the couple walking across from us were French from their mannerisms and way of walking. She was shocked when they walked closer, and we heard them speak English in a British accent!

So, leaders can recognise that even if they convince themselves that something is right, a better option can be something quite different. So, if someone else has a different opinion, it might just be that there is something that the leader might have missed. In that sense, they are open to change.

I do believe there is an additional level that few leaders genuinely embody, but which can be incredibly empowering for a whole organisation. This is the understanding that the world is a subjective existence, and so it is not even clear that there are 'right' and 'wrong' answers in the first place.

When making decisions, the more important part is to genuinely understand what the objective is. This is going further than a benign statement such as 'make more money' or 'become more efficient'. It goes into the depths of *how* and *why* a team should approach a solution in one way rather than the other.

By taking the time to explore this with people, it can boil down to what values they are following by making a decision.

To take the example of 'make more money'. The approach of the leader may be to make money in the most efficient way possible. This is as they are being judged upon their team's key performance indicators. As they are ultimately being held accountable for the results, this is the bottom line for them. They may be a conscientious leader that also cares about their team, so this would also come into their consideration too, but perhaps as a lower priority.

A front-line team member however may feel very differently. They may be people-oriented and may want to ensure that what they are doing is genuinely helping the customer, rather than pushing for a sale that they know the customer does not need. Although this person has a key performance indicator on their head, their day-to-day conversations are with people. They would much prefer to help rather than focus on upselling.

Embodying an active diversity champion

I recently went to a museum in the South of Italy. It looked a bit quiet in there, but we had some time spare. We popped in. The cost of the entry ticket was 8 euros, with a concession ticket of 3 euros. The lady there asked us if we were students, were under 25, or had any other reason to get a concession.

She explicitly asked several times, though unfortunately for us, we had to pay the full price. When we entered the museum, it was small, bare bone and rather underwhelming. The downstairs had been closed due to flooding and the exhibition was predominantly a random assortment of artefacts. There was a high pitch noise coming from an alarm, which made it unpleasant to stay for too long.

We did not stay for too long and left feeling short-changed. Having worked in a museum before, the reaction of the lady did suggest to me that she did not believe it was worth the 8 euros they charged for entry.

People who work at museums also tend to be lovers of history and would much prefer that as many people come in to learn about history than necessarily making as much money as possible.

However, someone working on managing the budget of the organisation would not get these nuances of this experience. Instead, for them, the key would be to ensure that there was enough to keep the lights on as well as make a profit.

Neither of these perspectives are necessarily 'right' or 'wrong'. But they are different, and both have value. The magic comes when these different realities are combined to find one that serves the different priorities of a whole team, rather than those who are more senior, or ultimately the one that makes the most money for the organisation.

If there was more love put into the museum with a better organisation of the exhibition, along with a potentially lower price, I think that would benefit all stakeholders by attracting more people to come, who would learn more about the history of the region whilst also providing more money to the organisation.

So, embodying a genuinely inclusive approach is understanding that the different realities people have are equally correct. They are simply looking at reality from a different pair of eyes. By bringing together these views, a team is no longer trying to find who is more 'right', but instead collecting different views and considering them equally.

Now, that does not mean to say that a decision is therefore going to be popular with everyone. Ultimately, a decision will depend on what the goal is, which requires a choice of what is more important. But by gathering views across different people, it allows a much wider set of perspectives than would have existed otherwise.

This will allow a team to get a much more holistic view when making a decision. Whilst the decision-making process therefore can take longer to consult, it ultimately works out better by avoiding choices based on who can speak the most eloquently or is the most powerful in the room.

Where does diversity come into how people think?

There is something that can feel contradictory when talking about diversity and inclusion in such broad terms. On the one hand, we are talking about inclusive leadership – where we want to take a broad approach to how we respond to anyone in essentially the same way – coming from love and kindness.

It can be easy to get in a tangle - if we want to live by basic values of trust, love and understanding, do we need to go into the issue of diversity? After all, we're all human, and if we treat individuals with courtesy and respect, does it matter where they come from?

I do not see a contradiction. Whilst I want to treat every individual I meet with love and respect – whether I agree with them or not – I also want to be openly curious and understanding of their perspective. If we take a blanket approach to being 'nice', this will quickly fall into our definition of what acting nice is.

When I am back home with my parents, my idea of 'nice' is eating my mum's cooking (whether I am full or not!) but doing that as a guest at a friend's house might be rude. My mum asking if I want to have lunch at 11am when I come back home is her version of nice too. For me a bit less so.

People have different lived experiences. Taking a diversity lens is viewing the issue as the common experience that someone might have as a result of their upbringing. Someone who has grown up as a black male in an impoverished neighbourhood is statistically far more likely to be involved with gangs than a white woman growing up in an affluent suburban background.

Furthermore, if a black male's representation in the media is overwhelmingly negative, this can be a shared experience across that entire group. If we then go on to talk about our views on the media (or institutional organisations more broadly), from this perspective it would be unsurprising to see a greater level of suspicion from a black male.

By approaching our conversation from a place of openness and genuine curiosity, we can learn how these influences can shape a person's life. If we talk to many people across a group and find a similar issue being raised, this suggests that there is a wider problem. Some might be relatively well known, such as the negative portrayal of black men in the media, but others, such as the lack of black male role models might be something we were not aware of.

To take an explicit example, I was in a conversation with colleagues about issues within the LGBT+ community. By being openly curious to learn, he learnt that there was a pretty evident case of racism. My colleague had no idea that it was an issue – he innocently assumed that being a part of a minority group would mean that such issues would not exist due to a greater level of tolerance.

Now, if we were expected to already know about every single issue in each subset of marginalised individuals, we would have an overwhelming and impossible task. However, if we take an open approach to learning more about the experiences of different people, we can learn a great deal in a relatively short amount of time. So, the emphasis is less on knowledge, and more on openness to learn.

It's also important to recognise that an individual may have had different levels of exposure to an issue such as racism, sexism or homophobia depending on their circumstance, and they may also have a completely different reaction to it.

The way we react to something is based on our thoughts. This helps explain why certain individuals from a minority background may respond with disillusionment to the system, but other people from the same background may respond by looking to make things better. In other words, we can accept there is an inherent unfairness in the system, that still gives space for how an individual from a disadvantaged background responds to it.

A great influence for me early in my career was hearing successful ethnic minority speakers. They did not hold back on the details around issues they faced – a difference in pay compared to their colleagues, implicit messaging around their career potential or having no role models to support their growth.

However, they also recognised that this was the reality of their situation, so they could either sit in despondency, or they could make it work by finding a different path or putting in more effort than their peers. Often, they would describe that they used it as a source of motivation to prove their worth, rather than using it as a reason that they could not succeed.

We get to choose the narrative.

How to help someone from a different background

It can be tempting to simply tell people that they should change the way they think about their situation. But this can often come across as obnoxious and fail to recognise an understanding of the situation.

I have had situations in my career where I have had a white male senior explain to me why I should think differently about something without self-awareness that they had not gone through the experience I had. This also did not appreciate the point that me following their advice would probably have negative repercussions compared to them as I would be viewed differently.

At the same time, we can still help people. How can we help someone from a marginalised group who might be falling into a victim mentality?

Well, the first thing to say is that it's hard for us to change how other people think. I believe that's probably a good thing – after all, who are we to decide who is right or wrong? I do not think it would be morally right to tell someone to think differently if they feel resentful that they have been overlooked for a job for 20 years. They could be right that the situation is indeed unfair.

So, I find the best way to start is to genuinely understand where an individual is coming from. If they have grievances, take the time to genuinely listen to them. All too often leaders do not take the time to understand the perspective of people raising issues, and this can quickly turn into a culture of clamping down on dissent. Understanding why they feel the way they do gives a solid foundation.

From this, I find it helpful to set out examples of how things like how I frame the world have benefitted my understanding. When I take a non-advice-giving approach, I can simply share my own story to see if it helps the other person. For example, when I had an issue with a person in my team feeling inferior for being a woman from a working-class background, I did not have that direct experience to help her.

However, I did have things that I found helped me in terms of dealing with issues where I felt like an outsider, for example by focusing less on what people were thinking and more on the outcome. I usually offer these stories as prompts rather than direct advice – I recognise that I do not have the answers to the issue

131

the person in front of me has. However, what I do have is my own life experiences that can be beneficial. It then allows the other person to take the message I am sharing if it's helpful, or not if it's not applicable. After all, I could be misunderstanding their concerns.

Once we have shared our insights, we can see whether this is helpful for them. As mentioned previously, it is ultimately the other person's choice on how they think and feel about the issue. It's best to avoid the territory of telling people how to feel (for example, have the words 'you need to calm down' ever actually made anyone calm down?).

This approach requires a few things. Firstly, it requires genuine authenticity. If you're making up a story to make a point, people will smell the BS from a mile away. So, the story must be an honest one that comes from the heart.

Secondly, it requires a level of comfort in talking about our own experiences and talking about how we may have felt in a situation. This is the vocabulary we might not have learnt yet. The good news is that we can learn to increase our emotional vocabulary and comfort in openly talking about ourselves. Acclaimed writer and speaker Brené Brown in 'Dare To Lead'[23] talks about vulnerability being leadership, and that is the case here.

Thirdly, you will require some level of experience that will help this person with their issue. This may sound intimidating when you do not know how to deal with an issue such as discrimination. Here's more good news – you already have the experience you need to help someone.

Whilst life may feel complex when we go into the details, ultimately much of what we think and feel is not unique. We've all had that feeling when we've seen something unfair, and we've all gone through some period of sadness, anger, or stress. These are not unique emotions, and the person you may be talking to is ultimately feeling something you have felt before. Sometimes they just need to hear how it was for you.

I did an exercise recently of thinking about what I would say to a past version of myself. I remembered how stressed I would get ahead of my managerial

[23] Brené Brown, *Dare To Lead* (2018)

meetings – I was not particularly happy with the way we were doing things, or how I was being treated in the team. I would spend so much time being anxious about them that I would play out how I would want the conversation to go. I thought about all the 'hard truths' I could say to them.

By the time I got to the meeting, I found myself tired and jaded. I was grumpy before the meeting had even begun. Unsurprisingly, the meetings were not particularly fun. All the conversations that I had dreamt up in my head flew out the window once I had the person in front of me holding a real conversation rather than the pantomime I imagined in my head.

I would perhaps say to my younger self that putting negative thoughts on a situation leads to it being negative before it has even started. I would probably explain how I learnt that you do not need to react to all the thoughts and feelings that come to you and that ultimately in a year this meeting which feels so important right now you probably will not even remember.

Life experiences can be very valuable, and these are things that you already have inside you. Yes, it's helpful to go out and learn more things by picking up a meditation book or learning the latest thinking on how we can manage stress. But ultimately, if you've gotten this far in life you've probably got enough things to help another person, whatever their background.

So, if done in the right spirit, you can help them by sharing your own experience. This is most powerful when you can demonstrate that you follow the things that you would suggest to someone else for yourself.

Leading by example

Leading by example is a term we use regularly, but how many of us do it?

It is much easier (and fun!) to tell other people what they should do compared to doing it ourselves. Much of the disconnect between employees and their leadership is when the culture is 'do as I say, not as I do'.

I was speaking to a friend recently about this. They started a new job and they were told that the workplace was open to new ideas. However, they were swatted off any time they ever brought something new to the table. The leadership liked the idea of saying they were open to different ideas, but the truth was very different

Following on from the last chapter, supporting an individual from a disadvantaged background can feel daunting, however, in its essence, there are many ways we can support them.

But for this to be truly powerful, we can demonstrate that we walk the walk. For example, if there is a higher rate of mental health issues in a team which is affecting those from disadvantaged backgrounds (which is statistically usually the case), leaders often may respond to this by saying that people should feel free to take breaks from work or go for a walk.

Whilst this is nice, I recall many leaders talking about how these things have been beneficial for them, but they have not done them for quite a long time since they got too busy. Whilst the intention is good, this demonstrates that a problem is for the individual to sort out for themselves.

A more powerful response would be to demonstrate that caring for wellbeing and mental health is a priority for you as an individual and as a team. If you can lead the way by taking breaks and leaving the office at a reasonable time, it can go a long way to setting a culture where such actions are permissible.

After all, if you are a leader, you are probably the most visible person in the team. This shift may sound difficult, but if you make it, you will see the massive benefit of reduced burnout and higher wellbeing. This is what makes the difference to happy workplaces that have greater productivity.

I have been in several roles where I manage people, and I recall a conversation about how it was important to have honest feedback. One of my colleagues casually mentioned to me unprompted that they liked how I approached my management because I was willing to give direct feedback, but I also was willing to take it as well. This made it far less personal and made them more comfortable saying what they thought.

On a wider organisational level, I remember working in government when the Black Lives Matter protests took place. I was fortunate to be in an organisation that had already taken great strides in opening the conversation on race. As such, the response from leadership was sensitive, clear, and honest. Each Deputy Director was asked to have conversations on how people felt about it within their teams and to report this back up the chain afterwards.

The feedback was put together and set in an organisational response. The response itself talked about the importance of tackling race, but it also highlighted that this had been a priority for the department for several years.

Rather than a knee-jerk launch of new initiatives, it was looking to continue the work that had already been ongoing and to bring it into greater focus within the organisation. It was genuinely impressive leadership, and it was no wonder that our department was often referred to as a pioneer across government departments in how it dealt with sensitive issues, particularly on race.

Leading by example is an extremely powerful tool. It's probably not the first time you've heard the term, but it can be particularly effective when driving change within the organisation. You do not need to be from a marginalised community or a disadvantaged background to lead on these issues.

The opposite is the case. Without leaders from the majority groups, it puts all the pressure on the people who do already have additional hurdles to also be the providers of solutions and leadership. For instance, I had a black Deputy Director who would get asked to do so many interviews to make up a diverse

135

panel I had no idea how she was also meant to do her job! Practising what you preach is extremely powerful. The best bit is that it will also make you a better, and more impactful leader.

VI.   What organisations can do

We've spent some time understanding what Diversity means for you and how we might embody it in our day-to-day lives. This chapter looks at what sort of actions organisations can take to address the issues.

Creating a diverse and inclusive organisation does not happen magically, and so there is a critical role for organisations to proactively put in place measures to make it happen.

This chapter in particular highlights good ways for organisations to tackle the issue. Unfortunately, many well-intentioned methods can cause more issues rather than fix them.

As such it is critical to take a pragmatic approach which is both action-oriented but also reactive to the sensitivities and nuances the subject can bring. This is particularly challenging when taking this approach is not the norm in an organisation.

This chapter explores systems approaches in more detail.

What organisations can do by implementing a D&I Strategy

A growing number of modern organisations now have a diversity and inclusion Strategy. These are ways in which the organisation commits to building greater diversity and inclusion.

The quality of these strategies varies – whilst some organisations genuinely are looking to create a diverse and inclusive culture, others are often set out purely for the sake of having a strategy to avoid criticism.

Most organisations are somewhere between these two extremes. There is a general will to do something about it, but a mixture of lack of experience, resourcing and active implementation means this is ineffective. Many organisations struggle with the change management aspects involved –systemic barriers require a revisiting of the whole process in which an organisation works. This requires time and commitment to make changes.

The best diversity and inclusion strategies are deeply embedded within the wider business strategy. That way, it is seen as mission-critical and is not the first thing to fall away when budgetary pressures or management changes come along.

As this book is not focussing specifically on diversity and inclusion strategies, we will not go too in-depth here. Nonetheless, it is helpful to get a general idea of what a diversity and inclusion strategy should cover.

Recruitment

Organisations often start with a relatively homogenous workforce. Statistically, they may find that they have an underrepresentation of women, ethnic minorities, disabled and LGBT+ staff. A natural starting point is looking at the talent coming through the doors. How many staff from diverse backgrounds are making it to an interview? Are they even applying in the first place? Understanding the pipeline will help understand where the blockages are. It is then possible to take remedial measures.

For example, if there is a lack of BAME applicants applying, more outreach can be done to areas with a high BAME population. If you are then finding many are not making it to an interview, look at your job adverts and see whether your requirements are genuinely open to people with different experiences or have been written in a way that has a certain type of person already in mind.

Inclusive Culture

You may have improved your recruitment practices, what happens then? Getting staff from different backgrounds through the door in itself is not the solution – if your organisation does not make any shift to the culture or already be inclusive, what you often find ensuing is some level of disharmony within the workplace.

Often where there is only one BAME or woman staff in the team with little effort to integrate them, it can be very easy for these individuals to feel the odd one out. And whilst we would love to simply expect people to adapt to the people around others from whatever background, the reality is that we naturally gravitate to those who are like us.

We need to genuinely make our workplaces inclusive, where it is open as possible for anyone from any background to come in and thrive. Culture takes time to change and requires senior leaders to genuinely bring these conversations and hear people's stories to start the conversation.

Some smaller wins include making team socials more inclusive (e.g., having breakfasts as well as the usual pub visits to include more people); build staff networks within your organisation to allow groups to come together and share experiences. Another example is making your working practices as flexible as possible in terms of working hours and being output focussed on performance management rather than hours spent at the desk.

Retention and Progression

One area to be wary of is diverse staff joining and then quickly leaving the organisation. This can be very frustrating when a lot of effort has been put into bringing these people in. Without genuine inclusion, people will often feel excluded and will look to the door rather than stay in the organisation.

What often happens in an organisation is women and staff from BAME backgrounds tend to get stuck at the bottom. Often there are issues relating to pigeon-holing abilities of people with unconscious bias at play. Individuals are type-cast as unable to progress due to not having 'leadership traits' which are often built in the mould of its founders, rather than allowing different styles of leadership in.

Lack of opportunities is often cited as an issue, particularly for BAME staff. It would be a good idea to monitor how such staff are feeling about their prospects to get a good litmus test on how your D&I strategy is working.

Data

Data is paramount to understanding what is happening within organisations. If you cannot understand why people are leaving within a year, it is vital you go figure it out. To successfully monitor a D&I strategy, you may need to overhaul your current HR systems with the ability to properly monitor application rates from different backgrounds. Exit interviews are also a vital way to understand why employees are leaving and an opportunity for genuinely honest feedback.

Engagement

We've all seen dozens of strategies pass through our inboxes. Most of them are simply glanced over and little due regard is paid to them after a week or two.

So, getting staff genuinely engaged in what you are trying to do is critical. Building your support structures within the organisation through volunteers that are enthusiastic about the cause is vital. Also, remember that much of this strategy will be delivered by managers across the organisation, so if you have done little to tell them what they need to do, the chances of it happening are slim.

One final reflection is that there is no one-size-fits-all solution to a good diversity and inclusion strategy. Each organisation will have its different strengths and challenges. It is critical for firms to look at their own situation and build a realistic ambition of where they would like to further improve.

Tackling issues around inclusion

I have worked in several different teams, often led by 'good' people who generally work hard, are considerate, and have no explicit ill-meaning malice within them. So why does it often go so wrong?

The teams that I often worked in were created at a very quick pace due to wider work pressures and the fast-paced nature in which business demands are changing quickly. Realistically, this trend is unlikely to change, with our working lives becoming more embroiled in shifts and rapid changes, organisations are becoming more agile in deploying teams quickly to respond to new opportunities or challenges.

Unfortunately, when teams are built up at pace, often little thought is put upon team dynamics and building a wider inclusive culture. And whilst nobody sets out to build a non-inclusive culture, this aspect falls through the cracks as lots of new managers grasp to understand their new responsibilities. They instead are focused that they are delivering to their job standards and proving they can do the job. This can quickly turn into command-and-control decision-making from the top.

Organisations do not help themselves in how they set up these teams. Generally, highly proficient individuals are selected to lead the team. This is potentially on promotion, rewarding these individuals for their hard work and their technical potential rather than management capacities.

Unfortunately, there is usually little focus on new-found management responsibility or the importance of building a team. As such, what often takes place is a strong technical deliverer (but average manager) gets promoted into a position of responsibility where they are suddenly the head of dozens of people or more. With little training and guidance around this area (or even considering whether someone would be a good team leader from a people perspective in the first place), the seeds are sown for a poor team culture.

What often happens is that the new team leader operates in the same way that they did when managing a small team. This is particularly problematic because the way of working with a few people is very different to managing a large group of people. Whilst things like relying solely on informal conversations through coffee point chats or at the pub are less of an issue when it is a group of three, it does not work for a team of 20. Instead, what it leads to is those with direct access via these methods are thrust into a position of exclusive access to decision-making.

Others outside of this group find it difficult to get their voice heard. Staff instead must resort to turning up where their boss does to be 'seen' or for any of their ideas to see the light of day.

This also plays out in teams that have the opposite dynamic – these teams were built many moons ago and are stagnant vessels drifting at sea. Rules were set long ago, and little is done to necessarily bring change. Here, the set rules are difficult to challenge, and the shots are usually called by those who have been in the organisation the longest.

Leaders are inadvertently creating an exclusive culture. It requires a good deal of introspection and thought for leaders to take stock of routes of access, and how relying on traditional communication methods (i.e., hierarchical messaging upwards) is fraught with the danger of them only hearing one side of the story from the people they interact with frequently.

This leads to problematic decision-making due to a disconnect with what is happening throughout the team and leads to growing disillusionment and resentment from wider staff who are not part of the more exclusive club.

This usually manifests itself via worse employee engagement and satisfaction scores, leading to middling output. Higher staff turnover and its associated cost to the business are usually the results. It can also lead to siloed work and a lack of attention in all areas of a project.

For example, areas such as team or project management, HR or finance may just get side-lined despite being critical functions. In all, there is little positive to come out of an exclusive culture.

Leaders can look to re-evaluate how accessible they are to the whole team. One idea is having 'open hours' for anyone to speak with them anonymously about issues they may be having. Leaders could also go a step further and try and book short catchups with more junior members of the team to get a better sense of the mood music from below.

Leaders can also look to build more inclusive habits in their meetings, ensuring more equitable participation from different people. They can also look to break down implicit hierarchical barriers by empowering more junior staff to give their opinions at regular intervals.

From an organisation's perspective, much can be done to avoid the negative culture being built in the first place. Organisations can do much more to value, train and assess management capability within their performance management, and when looking at promotions or job opportunities for their staff.

Currently, organisations rarely consider whether people are likely going to be good at leading a team when putting them into a post, despite it being a critical factor in its success. An important way to do this is by instilling the importance of management and effective team working within their company values so that this is fostered throughout the whole organisation.

Further exploring an inclusive culture

An inclusive culture is where all people can feel comfortable discussing issues outside of the work context should they choose to. In a previous role, I wrote out a set of practical actions on how an organisation can create an inclusive culture. Inclusion is built through actions that are both at the micro and macro level.

1. Set out a team code of conduct which demonstrates a common level of respect for all individuals, no matter their background. Ensure new members actively view and agree to the code of conduct, and that this is reviewed regularly (e.g., every 3-6 months)

2. Individuals across the team are encouraged to role model positive behaviour and openness to discussions about backgrounds. This is because it makes conversations much easier if leaders and managers are open about their background before asking about it from their employees; moreover, it can help disarm the more threatening elements of questions ('where are *you* from'?)

3. Create safe spaces to discuss backgrounds and open conversations. For example, some teams hold lunch'n'learns where individuals can talk about their backgrounds in an open, curious, and non-judgmental manner. Another example would be to hold coffee chats (virtual or non-virtual) where people get to know each other and learn more about each other's backgrounds.

4. Create an environment where employees with disabilities and long-term health conditions feel able to come forward and discuss their disability, and any reasonable adjustments that they might need. Avoid making assumptions about their condition and ask them to explain how they experience it and what support, or reasonable adjustments they need. On top of practical considerations such as building/software assessments, it is key that this goes passed an HR issue to one where it is also how the team functions.

5. Ensure that conversations and social activities are inclusive as far as reasonably possible. E.g., holding 'breakfasts' as well as the usual pub gathering to allow parents or carers to attend. Ensure you include everyone as much as possible in work-related discussions and avoid 'water-cooler'

decision-making, where decisions are made when only certain people can be present. This can be particularly problematic when e.g., work discussions are being held around the men's toilets effectively leaving out all women.

6. Create clear mechanisms to deal with discrimination, and/or bullying and harassment within your team. Ensure that such mechanisms are used properly and are not simply viewed as a 'tick-box' exercise. Many organisations unfortunately have little way to actively deal with these issues, making it tough for it to be addressed within an organisation. This can be through the effective use of countersigning mechanisms or an anonymous 'agony aunt' style point of contact to raise issues within the team.

7. Where appropriate, at an individual level be naturally curious about other people's backgrounds and take an interest in what other people do outside of work. This does not mean going out and putting people on the spot about race, disability, or sexuality, so it is better to do it in an informal setting rather than a team meeting – e.g., many LGBT+ may feel uncomfortable being asked about their background and personal circumstances. Ensure that any questions are respectful and done in a positive spirit, respecting your colleague's response.

8. If you are not sure how to refer to someone, <u>ask them how they would like to be referred to</u>. There are many ways individuals can identify themselves, and it is worth remembering that 'BAME', 'LGBT+', 'disabled' etc. is a very wide umbrella – with many not being fond of the term 'BAME' or 'LGBT+': often people may prefer to be referred to as 'Black', 'Queer' 'Asian', 'neurodiverse' or something completely different. As there is no one-size-fits-all, the best way to do this is to ask. Once again, this is probably best done in a private conversation rather than in front of many other people.

9. Ensure you are following the basics of line management: scheduling regular one-to-one conversations, and performance development meetings and allotting sufficient time where possible. Ensure you are being fair and consistent in the amount of time and attention you give to your different staff – whilst this sounds obvious, in a study, research demonstrated only 20% of

women BAME respondents below senior management stated they received help from their line managers. In stark contrast, 75% of white women stated their continued growth was due to having a supervisor, champion, mentor or coach. Other examples I have heard have related to white managers not giving critical feedback to their ethnic minority staff for fear of being called a racist. The practical result was that they were getting less feedback and support from their managers compared to their white peers.

10. Encourage team members to actively take up informal roles on wellbeing, diversity or becoming reverse mentors, and for your seniors to sign up to be reverse mentored (reverse mentoring is further explored in a later chapter). If you feel comfortable doing so, gently remind your seniors to fulfil any objectives they have relating to diversity and inclusion or wellbeing.

11. Sign up for your organisation's staff networks (sometimes referred to as employee resource groups). Join as many networks as you'd like, even if you do not come from the characteristic of the group in question! It is important that the networks gain a wide membership to ensure their reach is across the organisation so do not feel afraid to join! If you do not have a staff network, why not create one?

Organisations with a strong culture of inclusion tend to do these activities. Nonetheless, it is still important to review and ensure that this is taking place regularly and systematically.

Diversity and Inclusion for small businesses

Much of our focus has been on the actions of large, multinational organisations and what actions they are taking. This does make sense, after all, they have the larger market shares and influence, as well as the resources to genuinely drive better standards in this area.

But what about small businesses? After all, in the UK, of the nearly 6 million total business population, 99% are Small and Medium Enterprises (SMEs). Much of the work of D&I practitioners focus on culture change for large organisations, meaning that smaller businesses are left without much guidance or support that benefits their needs.

I have spoken to some local businesses about this. Some of the issues related to a lack of resources to engage with the subject, a lack of expertise in this area or what to do in their regional location where there is less diversity in general. On top of this, simply surviving during COVID has taken been one of the most difficult battles for many local businesses, meaning additional aspirations on this agenda can be tough to justify.

It is worth stating that many of the strong business reasons for D&I apply to small businesses as well.

Serving diverse customers is a way to diversify business revenues. Offering products and services for underserviced communities can open additional opportunities for a local business. SMEs are particularly well placed to work closely with communities compared to larger businesses and serving a new neighbourhood could be a critical new revenue stream.

Customers have a growing societal conscience around diversity and inclusion, the environment and sustainability. People may be put off taking services if they feel a business is not representative or is not taking action to support the agenda. This is particularly important for community-based businesses.

If we frame this as an opportunity, the idea of working with a small local business is far more attractive than a big corporation, particularly when they can demonstrate an ethical view towards key issues.

We also cannot forget that the benefits of an inclusive culture still make an impact no matter the size of an organisation. For example, by creating an inclusive culture, businesses make people feel more comfortable working there. Happy staff = productive staff (and less turnover).

Attracting wider talent pools will help small organisations get the best talent available. This is particularly critical for small businesses in ethnically diverse areas that may not otherwise attract individuals from different backgrounds, and those requiring highly skilled talent such as tech firms.

It's also not all doom and gloom for small businesses in being able to act in this area. After all, small businesses are nimbler, and much more likely to be connected to their local community, giving them a closer insight into the local diaspora and are better able to build genuine relationships with key community leaders for different groups.

Multinationals on the other hand have a hard time getting passed being seen as 'faceless', and shifting priorities mean community relations can often fall by the wayside. Likewise, it is far easier to shift the internal inclusive culture of a small business, compared to a large organization employing thousands of people.

So, with this in mind, I have created a list of actions small businesses may want to consider. These are intentionally bitesize to consider limited resources, as well as the relative strengths small businesses have:

1. Have you asked how your employees feel? Have you asked them what it is like to work in your business? How do they feel about diversity and inclusion?

2. As a small business, you are likely already well-linked to your local community groups. Explore these avenues further to get a better understanding of what potential customers are out there, and what needs are currently not being met for them. Take a particular look at those from different backgrounds you may not have considered before.

3. Review your promotional material and website. How representative are they of different groups of people? Would they appeal to these groups?

4. See where you are advertising. Is there a way you can diversify your approach, e.g., getting in contact with the local mosque, diverse community groups, ethnic diaspora local newspapers etc.?

And if you would like to go a step further, take time to see how diversity and inclusion can be incorporated within your wider business plan and strategy. As highlighted above, this can play a key role in demonstrating a conscientious, ethical business that will also attract new customers.

Tackling gender pay gaps

Many countries hold their 'Equal Pay Day'. This is the day in which figuratively women stop earning compared to men due to the gender pay gap. In the UK, this was announced to be 18 November 2021 – based upon the fact that the gender pay gap is 11.9% in the UK. Other European countries such as France, Germany, Spain, and Belgium also mark this day, all of which tend to fall around the first few weeks of November. The European Commission marks the 10 November as the European Equal Pay Day – based upon an average of 14.1% lower pay compared to men.

Whilst, in theory, men and women legally are expected to be paid the same amount for the work they do, in practice this does not lead to the egalitarian society that we might hope for. Women are often passed up for promotion to senior levels or are undervalued for the work they do. Stereotypes still exist around the type of work women are capable of, meaning many organisations still do not see women as leaders or typecast as secretaries.

Some high-paying fields such as engineering and IT are heavily represented by men which further skews the balance. Likewise, the gender pay gap also highlights unbalanced societal norms, where childcare is expected to be covered by women, whereas this is not expected of men. Similarly, the figure can also be further skewed by a low percentage of women participating in the workforce in the first place, meaning at times the situation can be starker than the figure itself shows.

Whilst Gender Pay Gap is a wider societal issue, there is certainly far more that organisations themselves can do to tackle the problem. Unfortunately, the numbers have stayed consistent (and in the example of the UK went up), meaning that we cannot expect the passage of time to solve the problem. Instead, here are some suggested ways for organisations to approach the problem:

1. **understand own gender balance internally** – Organisations could do more to internally investigate their gender balance. A step further would be to start looking at whether there are pay disparities that have arisen over the years of promotions and salary negotiations. Some firms are now looking to correct these discrepancies by either offering top-ups to lesser-paid females at the

same grade, or by creating clearer salary bands which harmonise pay.

2. **maternity and return to work schemes** – Whilst generally we are seeing a balanced split of men and women entering the workforce overall in professional jobs, a large issue is women leaving work during pregnancy and maternity and not returning. This often places women having to choose between family and career, with corporate inflexibility making this feel like a binary choice. Organisations can do more to put in place return-to-work schemes, regular check-ins during maternity and better policies to support women as they go through maternity leave and encourage their return afterwards.

3. **Increase participation of women in sectors** – Certain sectors have systemic issues around the underrepresentation of women. A commonly cited example is the lack of female STEM (Science, Technology, Engineering and Maths) graduates, meaning there is a lack of representation in this space in the workplace. Organisations have looked at developing a better pipeline of staff by supporting girls' participation in these areas, for example through coding clubs or other initiatives. This does not just apply to technology though, but also to other sectors such as construction where more could be done to make girls feel this is a viable career pathway for them.

4. **reviewing internal culture** – It is vital that an organisation itself does not simply chase numbers of women, but instead also looks at how the organisation is run, and how genuinely inclusive it might be. Many organisations do not realise that their processes and work culture can be exclusionary for women. For example, in tech companies which are often male-dominated, they may have a drinking culture which may mean that a working mother is unable to progress due to not going for a drink after work due to childcare. They may not be seen as a 'team player' and are being passed up for opportunities.

5. **Shifting performance management and HR policies** – Organisations should review how they value their employees and see how they can make their workplaces more inclusive, for example introducing flexible hours and more options for part-time working and job-share roles. Importantly, those

who benefit from these schemes should also be seen as viable for promotion as well. Another practical way to tackle this is to support the creation of a women's network which can help women support one another within an organisation as well as advocate for more inclusive policies.

Staff networks (or employee resource groups)

Staff networks, or employee resource groups as they are sometimes called, are employee-led groups within an organisation. These are often based upon under-represented groups or protected characteristics, for example on race, LGBT+, Gender, Religion or Parental groups.

Since joining the office workforce, I have found staff networks an invaluable and critical function within the business organisation. So much so that I chaired the departmental race and faith network in one of my jobs for two years.

The reason staff networks are so valuable is that they are a force for genuine positive support and change within an organisation. In a world where we often bemoan hierarchical structures with little opportunity to have our voice heard, staff networks demonstrate a tried-and-tested way to bring the voice of different staff together and give them to the organisation as a critical friend.

With more emphasis and action towards diversity and inclusion, staff networks are often key sounding boards for HR initiatives that affect certain groups. For example, companies have spoken to their disability network to test products with a disability lens attached.

Staff within the company can see how well the product would work for disabled individuals and help ensure that accessibility features are in place. This is great for the organisation as it ensures a better-made product, whilst it also acknowledges and values the skills and experience that disabled staff have within the organisation too.

At their best, staff networks can go even further. In my time working as a network leader, I worked very closely with my HR to support, test and challenge new proposals, including introducing new talent schemes, performance management measures or outreach initiatives on recruitment.

In a space where HR budgets are tight, I could coordinate support via our volunteers to give valuable time and resources. Working in the Civil Service meant we had a wide range of expertise including analysts, policy professionals, and event managers, meaning we could tap into a rich and vast set of experiences that would otherwise be left hidden away in silos within the organisation.

We gave critical feedback to the head of our organisation on the situation around race, building a movement to highlight and address systemic issues. Using data and analysis, we presented across Senior Management Teams, eventually leading us up to the Executive Committee.

I was even given the space to present a paper with a set of recommendations to our top board (all of which were agreed upon). It's certainly not an experience I would have gotten without the recognition and creation of staff networks!

Bringing people together in support of an organisation by making people's voices heard is always an important thing to cherish. I do recognise that staff networks are often under-resourced or sub-optimally structured, however, we must remember that these are essentially a free resource for the business run by volunteers, and the amount they can bring to the table is far more than any set of external consultants trying to do the same thing (not to mention far cheaper too!)

If you're a member of an organisation with staff networks within them, I would encourage you to get involved. A lot of blood, sweat and tears goes into maintaining them, and there is always a need for more volunteers. It is a fantastic way of widening your network, understanding more about the organisation's objectives and allowing yourself to pick up wider leadership skills. If you are a senior leader, these can be a great opportunity to champion a cause by offering to lend a hand.

If your organisation does not have a staff network, this may be an opportunity to set one up within the organisation. By highlighting the invaluable role they can do within an organisation, it can greatly support a business in achieving its diversity and inclusion objectives, as well as be a key sounding board for wider initiatives.

If you would like to learn more about staff networks, a book I recommend is The Incredible Power of Staff Networks by Cherron Inko-Tariah MBE.[24] This sets out how to run a successful network and the many pitfalls that these groups can go through.

---

[24] Cherron Inko-Tariah MBE, *The Incredible Power of Staff Networks* (2015)

VII.   What you can do

Whilst organisational change is necessary, organisations are run by people.

They are run by you.

One of the biggest issues around large-scale approaches to diversity and inclusion is that the people in organisations do not understand or believe in them. Even if they do believe in them, they do not actively do anything about the issue.

This may be due to people not feeling it's their place, or that they are ill-equipped to deal with the issues.

This chapter will examine this issue and how you can play an active role, wherever you might be right now.

Where to start?

For something as big and overwhelming as institutional inequality, the task can feel particularly overwhelming. After all, who are we as individuals to shift entire organisational structures and political organisations?

Conversely, if we all take individual responsibility, we can enact massive change. The Black Lives Matter movement came about because individuals were willing to publicly decry a situation, which led to greater conversations and a social movement globally. The power of the individual is greater than we might realise.

There are many specific actions you can do to make a change in the world. Subsequent chapters will go into detail about what these things can be. Fundamentally though, the idea of being an advocate for diversity and inclusion is not about a textbook set of activities. It is actively exploring, raising, and finding solutions to issues without needing to be prompted.

This can take many different guises, but examples could be actively speaking to people within different ethnic groups or taking more time to welcome a new team member and value their perspectives. It is also being active and visible around issues of inclusivity.

For me, it was volunteering in numerous different initiatives in the workplace, posting about diversity and inclusion online and writing this book. This was my journey, but it may look very different to you.

In my last organisation, I recall that we had created 'champions' who were senior-level members of the organisation whose role was to actively empower and champion certain issues. We had one on diversity and inclusion. I recall that nobody even knew he had the title, suggesting that his effectiveness in the role was not particularly high. When he did give his views, they tended to be from a place of telling people what they should do. I recall chairing a staff network where his advice was that we do less and focus on only several priorities.

That makes for a nice piece of generic strategic advice, unfortunately, I never got to ask him what we should deprioritise. Since we were a network representing ethnic minorities and faith groups, I would have loved to have asked him who should be deprioritised out of the Muslims, Christians, Sikhs, and Jews. Or who was more important out of the ethnic minorities - Blacks or South Asians?

Unsurprisingly someone who had taken little to no interest in diversity issues for his whole career until he was chosen to be a D&I 'champion' was not necessarily the best person for advising strategically on the issue.

Instead, the most powerful advocates for diversity and inclusion were those who were willing to understand these issues and take the time to involve themselves. They did not need a formal title to do so, as they recognised that it was important for them as an individual to get involved. What often followed was them then getting approached to be diversity champions because people saw them as leaders.

I recall a white senior leader taking the time to come to our monthly staff network meeting, supported by a black member of staff within his team with the proposition of writing a blog from a white man's perspective on the need to talk about race. Although it took some time to get over the sensitivities, he ended up writing this blog.

What followed was one of the most shared and read blogs our organisation ever had, with over 2000 views in an organisation of around 4000 people. This launched a wave of activity as it had an accompanying survey which demonstrated that over 80% of people did not feel comfortable talking about race. This was what launched a massive amount of activity within the organisation to bring about great change.

The leadership demonstrated here was invaluable, and it took an individual who was willing to go out of his way to make it happen. It was unsurprising that we later asked him to be one of our champions, and he became an influential figure in this space across government.

Nobody told him to write a blog or to actively pursue the agenda of race. But he felt compelled to do so. He also understood that the traction he had gained presented a critical opportunity to change the organisation, so he took up the cause as our champion. This allowed him to advocate the issue at more senior levels. There was no textbook he was following on this, but there was the willingness to engage in whatever felt appropriate.

The point of this chapter is not to try and give a list of actions to take. Instead, it's about how you can shape yourself to be the person you want to be to actively advocate for diversity and inclusion in the world.

If you are committed to making change, you will find ways to make it happen.

Getting creative with solutions

Cookie-cutter solutions rarely work to 'fix' the issues, whether it be the representation of diverse groups at senior levels or creating a more inclusive environment.

Whilst there are schemes you may have heard of that might help such as introducing a talent track, reverse mentoring, or a sponsorship programme, these are not the silver bullet to creating the utopian organisations that our diversity and inclusion strategies envision.

Take the responsibility into your own hands. No external person will know your organisation better than you do. You understand what the aims and objectives are, the products it makes, and most importantly the way it works. Find ways for you to solve the problem. In other words, it's an opportunity for you to get creative.

Creative solutions do not need to be creating the next COVID vaccine, it can be as simple or effective as tweaking the staff rota. Do you have staff that have childcare responsibilities? Ask to see if someone else might prefer early morning starts and see if the parents can clock in later. Do people perhaps get turned off by the idea of a pub social every week? Why not take a meeting room and host a board game evening, or do breakfast/lunch socials instead?

These small acts can be very powerful in fostering better inclusion and wellbeing for staff, particularly those from diverse groups (or indeed anyone who is not a fan of noisy pubs, including some of the introverts!).

Whilst this may not sound like much, you are playing your part in creating that inclusive culture. Your strategy may talk of grand shifts in recruitment practices or hard-set targets, but it is your actions on the ground that will genuinely shift the culture which is so vital for success in this area.

Inclusive environments also tend to perform better. Whilst you may feel like you are not doing much, you may be role-modelling positive behaviour, and sooner or later you will be looked at with envy by other teams and departments. Your staff will laud the positive practices you initiate, and often others can quickly copy and follow suit. This grassroots, more spontaneous style of improving workplace culture will trump any boardroom-approved strategy mandating people to do so.

Embrace your creative side to solve some of the diversity issues you face, and there is no need to feel intimidated by the word 'creative'! I have recently reflected that I am far more creative than I previously believed.

I always thought of 'creatives' as coolly dressed artists with a pencil and notebook in hand all the time. I never thought of creativity as a skill, rather than creative being a word used to describe a musician, artist, or writer. It turns out I have a natural knack for creative problem-solving, which I never even thought of as something I was good at.

Come with a fresh pair of eyes and perhaps ask yourself – 'what have I not yet considered?'

Taking a coaching approach

Many are aware of the benefits of mentoring, both for personal development and for advising on diversity and inclusion. Coaching, however, is usually more misunderstood; and whilst a growing amount of diversity and inclusion professionals may offer coaching-type services, this may often turn more towards mentoring where experience is predominantly shared. Although this is beneficial, it does not fully embrace the full positive benefits of coaching.

From my experience, coaching and diversity and inclusion go hand-in-hand. It is a way for individuals to come up with an understanding of the issue for themselves, as well as provide actions they can take from the point of view of their upbringing. It also makes the subject more accessible and can bring in views from those who do not have an obvious reason to be interested in D&I (e.g., being white, straight, abled etc.).

It was the primary reason I wanted to write this book, as I felt few people were harnessing the power of coaching when dealing with diversity and inclusion. D&I practitioners are often getting burnt out and find it difficult to get buy-in within the organisation. I have found that the magic is demonstrating why D&I is relevant for the individual, and how it can play into their own belief.

Coaching is extremely powerful as it allows individuals to come to their solutions, rather than being told what to do. It also allows us to bridge the gap between difference of experiences. I have previously reverse-mentored senior white leaders, and whilst this process was highly valuable for both of us, I was mainly describing experiences that the senior leader would find difficult to identify with directly. Reverse mentoring has an impact, though there is a further step to make it relevant.

I have since taken a coaching approach, and I have found this far more effective to overcome the obstacles they have around diversity and inclusion. For example, I recall working with one senior white leader who found this subject extremely frustrating and difficult to access: they cited the terminology constantly changing as an example of not knowing what to do. They also just simply did not understand the issue properly as they were not seeing it happen in

162

front of them. They were too senior to see this playing out on the ground – even if the statistics did prove that this was happening.

Through a coaching approach, I was able to dig deeper into their stumbling blocks around the subject, and give some prompts as to why this may be frustrating (which in this case was partly because it sounded like an attack on them in that they did not care about their staff, which was not the case) and over the process of time get more comfortable talking about diversity and inclusion for themselves. It also allowed them to bring their perspective and understanding of the subject.

By the end of the process, I found this senior leader became one of the biggest advocates for diversity and inclusion within the organization, and the outcome was far more effective than if I had taken an approach to constantly bang the drum to them about why diversity and inclusion were important.

I believe that diversity and inclusion practitioners (and indeed anyone advocating around the subject) would greatly benefit from taking a coaching approach, particularly when having a trusted relationship with seniors.

I believe it also better mimics how we as individuals got passionate about diversity and inclusion in the first place. For most of us, this required a real-world stimulus relating to an injustice we have witnessed or felt personally, which made us reflect on why inequalities are allowed to happen. Coaching allows us to give this experience to senior leaders who may not have experienced any of these issues, simply as they never saw it themselves.

I have all too often seen the passion of individuals around diversity and inclusion crossing over to becoming an impediment to positive change. Whilst positive energy is certainly needed to drive the agenda forward, many senior leaders can be put off or intimidated by practitioners.

Practitioners can come across as intense or are seen as one-dimensional if their approach tends to always be to challenge the organisation. What is lacking here is the supporting function to bring a leader who has little to no experience in this area into a space of awareness and allyship, something which coaching is extremely successful in doing.

If you are a senior leader looking to make a change in the organisation, this approach also is a great way to get other colleagues on board. It demonstrates how it is relevant for them. It is also particularly useful when you are mentoring a junior colleague who may come from a different background. For example, senior men often mentor junior women, stating that they should simply be more assertive in meetings. This fails to consider that women are judged far more harshly when they take a domineering position compared to men.

If you were in this situation, you could instead look to understand the issue through their eyes and come up with solutions that would be appropriate for them. In this case, this could be to approach people before the meeting to get agreement to your propositions so that they are supported within the meeting itself. I can recall senior white women talking about how they use this tactic to get around the issues they have faced and helped them gain traction in key boardroom meetings.

How to be 'agile' in addressing diversity and inclusion issues

With a growing professionalization in the space of diversity and inclusion, more can be done to use project management principles to improve the approaches (and thus the success) of diversity initiatives.

Agile is a project management approach, originating from software but is now commonly used in dynamic projects. This approach is different from common corporate planning approaches where the aim is to plan everything at the beginning, get approval from seniors and deliver the whole project in a 'big-bang' approach at the end, which tends to have low success rates as it is increasingly difficult to plan everything at the beginning in our uncertain environment.

Instead, Agile is about delivering in smaller iterations and being adept at changes. The Agile Business Consortium define Agile as being "able to move quickly and easily" or being "able to think and understand quickly".

The best diversity and inclusion champions have been those that have been willing to work smart. Admittedly, this has often been forced upon them – with shoestring budgets, supported by a disparate crew of motivated but voluntary individuals who can spare an hour here and there. But what is also evident is that this approach follows the basic principles behind an Agile mindset.

Those that are more successful in this space understand the importance of trying different initiatives quickly (and not being afraid to fail at them) as the approach can always be modified once you have learnt what has gone wrong.

Organisations often get stuck in getting the solution right the first time, thus spending months (if not years) agonizing over a potential solution. This leads to them both getting criticised for not acting, and when they finally do act, disappoint their stakeholders as the solution is a relatively small action in the end.

To get Diversity and Inclusion initiatives off the ground, here are a few principles I have found that tend to work (and which are inspired by an Agile mindset):

- Start small, and work to make the most of the resources and positive motivation you have available (even if that is only yourself or a handful of volunteers)

- It is better to start initiatives that fail rather than get stuck trying to find the perfect solution. You can learn from failure; you cannot learn from inaction.

- Accept you will get things wrong, such as using outdated words or definitions. Learn from your mistakes and correct them as you go along.

- Demonstrate value to the business and communicate how diversity and inclusion link to the overall business strategy constantly. This will help you get buy-in when someone may question why resources are being used in this space.

Whilst the above does take Agile's general principles, I also admit I do not reference a lot of other areas that are key to Agile (e.g., key roles and responsibilities, defined ways of working etc.) This is deliberate, as I believe that would come later when organisations are ready to put clearer resourcing into D&I work. For you as an advocate, the key approach is being resourceful.

As an aside, the skills I learnt by running a small group of volunteers were an incredible experience that greatly improved my professional competence in management and planning and also helped refine my personal beliefs and values. Although at times this work can be frustrating, it is also incredibly rewarding too.

Reverse mentoring

Reverse mentoring is a spin on traditional mentoring. Rather than the more senior, experienced person being the mentor, they are the 'mentee'. The more junior person is the one doing the mentoring.

The reason reverse mentoring is valuable is that it can connect established leaders who are often white to more junior staff who might be from a wider, diverse background. Even if they are both from the same ethnic group, it can serve to highlight the experiences of more junior staff in terms of issues around pay, inclusion and societal expectations which shift every generation.

The reason reverse mentoring is also particularly popular is that it is essentially a free resource. All it takes is a commitment from both sides to take time out to speak. For the senior mentee, it can give an invaluable insight into the organisation from a different lens and be one way to address the fact that they might not understand what is happening at junior levels. For the junior, it is a great chance to speak with senior leaders to better understand their priorities and what pressures they may be under, whilst also giving them critical exposure.

I reverse-mentored a senior white woman. In all honesty, she had a disability and was not that much older than me – she had climbed the ranks quite quickly. In broad terms, she understood the importance of diversity and generally was quite a vocal advocate.

Nonetheless, sharing my experiences helped her understand some of the pressures I had from a personal perspective relating to race and religion, as well as more broadly the challenges of being a more junior member of staff. I found it difficult to manage a healthy work-life balance at a point where I had not built the skills to develop healthy boundaries with my work, nor was I getting much support to do so either.

I also gained a lot in understanding how her pressures worked within the organisation. For me, someone who was two or three levels above seemed like an omnipotent being. Yet for her, she had pressures from her management and had to deal with a higher level of scrutiny. It certainly taught me one thing – in government, the hierarchy keeps going up!

What you can do

The scheme itself was organised by our HR team, who had a dedicated person who worked to match mentors and mentees. Since our Permanent Secretary – the most senior civil servant in the organisation - had personally used it himself and had advocated for it, we had a nice issue where we had more senior leaders wanting reverse mentoring than junior staff available.

The system can benefit from some level of training – the experience can be quite intimidating for a junior member of staff, so it is important to establish boundaries and levels of confidentiality around the process. Likewise, senior leaders should refrain from being overly judgemental or crossing the line in telling the junior person how to deal with their lives. Like any relationship, healthy boundaries are important for its success.

For the most part, reverse mentoring was nearly always a positive experience. When people came into it with the right intentions, it allowed for a pleasant, enlightening experience which did not have to be a conversation solely based on work. It is also a scheme that requires relatively little management and financial commitment from an organisation, which also helps make it so popular as it is relatively easy to implement.

If your organisation does not have a reverse mentoring scheme, you can create your version. This could include actively going out to speak with more junior staff or following the same principles in more informal conversations with them. Whilst having a central scheme helps to clarify the point of it all, there's no reason why you could not just replicate the aims of this for yourself.

Another option is to push for the creation of the scheme within your team or organisation. It is a relatively popular proposal due to the low cost, and it also serves as a tangible action for an organisation to implement when it looks to address diversity and inclusion.

Volunteering for a diversity leadership position

If you're looking for a way in which you can be more active, taking up a position can be an easy way to focus the mind.

Many organisations have diversity champions or advocates. This can be at a senior level, or simply a self-created 'lead' within a team. Having a position of responsibility can give you a clear way in, whilst also giving you legitimacy for working on the subject.

Sometimes people who are passionate about these issues feel uncomfortable with the idea of working on it during office time, however, the moment it is decided that this is something that they can do for the team it suddenly becomes an accepted practice.

For example, in one of the teams I worked in we created wellbeing leads. These leads, despite being relatively junior, now felt empowered to bring wellbeing issues to team meetings. This was accepted across the team once it had been established.

If you're in an organisation that already has a well-established organisational culture, you will likely find that there are lots of opportunities to volunteer for a cause. This could be as a champion of a group, to help with a voluntary project being created or simply with other corporate issues such as interviews and communications campaigns.

These roles are always difficult to fill, so anyone who comes with some level of enthusiasm is nearly always welcomed with open arms. I recall spending many months looking to find someone who could be our senior faith champion, which was something we did not have in the organisation.

It got to the point where we were a bit desperate, as we were eminently aware it was a role that had been empty for over a year. Meanwhile, race and gender were getting plenty of traction, leaving the issue of faith getting overshadowed. Fortunately, we did find someone (albeit at a less-senior level), which certainly helped.

If you do not see an opportunity within your organisation right now, do not forget that there are many voluntary activities you could also pursue outside of

169

work. Many charities and local organisations are always looking for support from professionals who can give strategic insight to them.

Alternatively, you can also look to create such voluntary positions for yourself. If you have been active on an issue like diversity for quite some time, you might simply want to ask whether it would be possible to legitimise it by making yourself a 'lead' or 'champion' for your organisation. This will give you additional visibility and legitimacy, whilst also supporting your own team's leadership by demonstrating that someone is working in this area.

Chairing inclusive meetings

We've all been in meetings which are decidedly un-inclusive. Whilst this is meant to be a 'team' meeting, 90% of the session is dominated by the chair, with very little input from anyone else.

So how can we avoid making our meetings a one-person band and instead one that is inclusive to the whole team? Here are some practical ways in which you can look to shift the culture of your team meetings, particularly as a chair. Even if you are not a chair, you can politely nudge your colleagues in this direction which will help instigate a cultural shift.

Before the meeting

The key to an inclusive meeting is usually preparation. After all, if you are sticking this in a time which does not work for most people (or indeed you've forgotten to even invite them) you are unlikely to get the full engagement you desire.

Things to consider:

- Is your invite list correct?
- Have an agenda, and ensure people can add points to an agenda ahead of time to keep it inclusive
- Is the date/time of the meeting one that is inclusive? E.g., avoiding school run times, or at unsociable hours for other time zones.
- Have papers been sent ahead of time?

During the meeting

Within the meeting, as the chair, it is your role to effectively facilitate the discussion. It is important to avoid abusing your chairing privileges which allow you to come in whenever you want, as this quickly leads to you dominating the conversation. Rather, if you do want to comment, perhaps open the floor for discussion first before giving your comment.

What you can do

As the chair is often the most senior person in the room, if they speak first, they are likely to stifle any discussion as more junior members of the team are less likely to want to disagree with what they say.

Things to consider:

- Try and make space for introductions – it makes any meeting far more human.
- Steer away from one / two people dominating the conversation (and avoid being one of those people yourself!). Be willing to kindly interrupt if someone is taking over. Agendas help with this as well to prompt a moment to move on to the next section.
- Use your ability as chair to ask others whether they would like to come in at regular intervals to ensure wider participation. Sometimes people need prompts before they come in.
- Give moments of pause to allow people to think before they are prompted with questions.
- Keep on time! If possible, invite reflections on the meeting at the end.

After the meeting

Whilst the meeting may be over, your job may not necessarily be done. Following up after the meeting can ensure everyone is clear with the tasks agreed upon, as well as a great opportunity to pick up more informal feedback from colleagues about how the meeting went.

Things to consider

- Send up follow-ups, actions, read-outs etc. Invite individuals to comment on the minutes.
- Check-in with individuals on how they found your chairing style and whether they got what they wanted for the meeting
- Finally, other things you may want to think about is having a rotating chair system, as well as a standing agenda point to review the meeting at the end. These both help increase engagement and give the team a greater sense of ownership over the meeting.

Diversifying your sources of information

One of the issues around diversity is that diverse voices are simply not being heard. Within an organisation, reverse mentoring can be one way to address that. But this principle can be applied more widely.

For example, it is worth looking at what sources of information you have. This goes for both your working and personal world. Is your main source of information predominantly coming from mainstream media? How many people on social media do you follow that come from different backgrounds than you? Are you getting information from your wider team, as opposed to only the most senior people around you?

There are a variety of things that you can do to change this. One thing that can make senior leaders more accessible to their teams is 'office hours', i.e., times when anyone can drop by to raise an issue or to have a chat. Even if you are not so senior, or you are not so keen on the idea of formalising it in quite that way, you can make it easier for people to approach you.

You can do this by highlighting within meetings that you are open to having a conversation with people, and actively taking an interest in the staff within your team. Whilst this may sound like a time investment, it will pay dividends when you are the first one to understand shifts in the mood within the office and have a clearer sense of the organisational struggles.

Outside of work, you can look to diversify the sources of information you are getting. Look to see if there are additional sources such as local newspapers or more diverse social media outlets or influencers who send a different perspective to our own.

As humans we tend to follow people who think and look like us, meaning we often develop echo chambers where we hear similar views to our own. It takes an active level of intentionality to break out of these bubbles and hear from different people. But doing so will give you a far richer set of information, and a greater understanding of political and societal changes. This can also be an edge that gives you an advantage when providing insightful views or information within team meetings.

Testing your group think

There is a useful exercise that can be effective in illustrating how much you may be susceptible to group think. Although we have been talking about group think from the perspective of our working lives, this also shapes our personal lives.

Imagine you are currently undergoing a rather large decision in life, perhaps whether to move to a new job, buy a new house or move countries. Take a moment and think about who your closest six friends or colleagues that you would ask for advice.

Once you have these six individuals, take a moment to identify the following attributes about them. If you are not sure, take a best-estimated guess:

- Age
- Sex
- Ethnicity
- Sexuality
- Nationality
- Location
- Level of education (e.g., university)
- Relationship status
- Have kids?

Once you have made a note of the six individuals, note whether there are similarities between most / all of them.

For me, although I have a good spread of people from different ethnicities, nationalities, sex and location, it becomes obvious that a lot of the people I would speak to are a similar age to me, are university educated, and in relationships but not married and do not have kids.

I believe I have quite a diverse set of friends having lived in a few countries, and yet when looking at it from this more thorough lens, I realised that a lot of people I would speak to have similarities to me. I have not added political leanings within this list, but on reflection, I imagine a lot of them would have similar views to mine as well.

More recently I have found that building greater friendships through connecting with other coaches has widened this pool. I now have people I could talk to who have not necessarily been to university, or are older and have kids. However, this would not have happened if I did not actively pursue ways to widen my friendship groups.

Now, there is nothing wrong with having friends like us. After all, we all have a preferential bias. The issue is when we use this as our exclusive set of friends, and do not reach out further afield to different people.

When making big life decisions, there are many perspectives that I simply would not get from the group of friends I would ask, for example thinking about settling later in life, and experiences around getting married or having children. However, without explicitly doing this exercise, which would not be evident to me, meaning I would be taking decisions following the advice of people that I previously thought was holistic!

Take a moment to look at your results. See where there are strengths in diversity, for example, if you live in a multicultural neighbourhood and have lots of friends from different ethnicities. This is also an opportunity to see the gaps in the sort of people you are asking, such as only asking exclusively male or female views.

This exercise is useful to identify when we may be subject to group think. In the workplace, we may have a similar phenomenon, particularly in a fairly homogenous environment. You may need to bring more expertise from different backgrounds – whether that be bringing in external expertise or ensuring decisions are including the different key stakeholders or departments.

At an individual level, you may want to look more widely at what your circles may be. You can then take action to expand them. One effective measure may be to review your own media consumption, in particular on social media. Have an audit of who you are currently following, and whether they may be predominantly white and male, which tends to be the case. Look at following people from different backgrounds who may give different and interesting perspectives you may not usually see. Likewise, try and find different news outlets, or get involved with a local community group. initiatives that may allow you to understand more about your locality from the eyes of a local ethnic group or community.

Like me, you could get involved in a new hobby which attracts a wider variety of people. Getting involved with local groups such as a sports team or attending a new dance class may be a good way to bring a greater variety of people from different backgrounds into your life.

When making decisions, try to ensure you have not assumed certain parts of information which may have an implicit basis. A regular coaching question can be 'what are we assuming here?' or 'what is the real issue we are dealing with?'.

An example was when I was coaching someone about needing to have a five-year business plan to succeed in their business. Whilst this may be a potentially helpful exercise, it also led them to overly focus on having everything planned out in a step-by-step process.

It is impossible to make a five-year plan without making assumptions about how the world might look. The issue is that things go very differently from how we might assume. None of us could have predicted a worldwide pandemic after all! This meant that less focus was being spent on the opportunities presented right in front of them, which may have been the more important conversation to have.

VIII.   Conclusion

Throughout this book, we have looked at what diversity means. The information from this book gives you the foundation to enter a conversation around diversity without feeling overwhelmed or confused. You may find yourself forgetting a few of the terms, but you can go back and refer to them in this book whenever you need.

But the aim of this book was not to simply give you information. It was also to give you the space to reflect on what this all means for you, as well as the tools to make change. Information only goes so far – this book instead is about transformation. I hope by reading this book you understand why you care about these issues, but also how you can make a change by the way you act in your day-to-day life. You can then supplement these with the tools and strategies that we discussed in the later chapters.

You can make a difference. Small actions build up to make substantial change. If you are open to it, I invite you to make a commitment, here and now.

Commit to an action that will make a difference, even if it is the smallest of tasks. This can be as basic as intentionally asking a colleague how they are tomorrow morning. Or it can be to commit to talking to someone from a completely different background to you. Whatever it is, commit to it. Make it happen.

Taking in the information you have read here will not change anything unless you do something with it.

The ball is in your court.

Conclusion

Final words

I wrote this book as a result of the Black Lives Matter movement. I recognised that I had built up sufficient knowledge around diversity and inclusion to genuinely help people understand more about the subject.

The book itself took a pause halfway through, simply because I ran out of things to say. I did not yet have the tools to go deeper. What followed has been an intense transformation of my own life based upon the coaching principles that I subsequently learnt about and formed in the later chapters. Once I had built a strong understanding of how we can transform as individuals (based on my own experience) I returned to finish this book.

So, I am delighted that a) this is now a completed book and b) that you have read this book. I wrote this with an intense desire to bring about positive change in the world. I saw a lack of resources for people who wanted to understand more about diversity and inclusion in an easily digestible way, whilst also giving the tools to people to understand it more for themselves. This book was my answer. I hope it has provided that for you.

If you've enjoyed reading this, I would love to hear from you. You can find me on Social Media:
https://www.linkedin.com/in/tahmidchowdhury1/
https://www.instagram.com/tahmid.chowdhury/
or via email at tahmid@chowdhury.co.uk.

QR code for my Linkedin:

Feel free to drop me a message, I respond to nearly everyone who sends me something.

I write a weekly newsletter which you can find on LinkedIn and my website – www.tahmidchowdhury.co.uk

Outside of my jobs, I work as a transformational coach which looks at the elements we've explored here, but also more broadly at how we live our lives. If you've found some of these concepts interesting or are keen to see how you could further your work in diversity and inclusion, I would love to speak to you. Having read this book, I am happy to offer you a complimentary coaching conversation. All you have to do is send me a message and we can take it from there.

Final Ask

If you have enjoyed this book, I would love for you to leave a review on Amazon. This will help people find this resource for themselves, and hopefully, help make a greater impact and change the world for the better.

If this book has helped you, I invite you to share it with a friend or colleague who you think might also benefit from it.

If you have any comments or questions, drop me a line at tahmid@chowdhury.co.uk

I look forward to hearing about the change you make in the world.

Tahmid

Further reading

Here are a small collection of books that have particularly influenced me which you may be interested in exploring:

Diversity

Caroline Criado Perez *Invisible Women: Exposing Data Bias in a World Designed for Men* (2019)

Charlotte Sweeney & Fleur Bothwick, *Inclusive Leadership* (2016)

Cherron Inko-Tariah MBE, *The Incredible Power of Staff Networks* (2015)

Reni Eddo-Lodge, *Why I'm No Longer Talking to White People About Race* (2017)

Coaching

Amy Hardison & Alan D. Thompson, *The Ultimate Coach* (2021)

Byron Katie, *Loving What Is* (2002)

Michael Neill, *The Inside-Out Revolution: The Only Thing You Need to Know to Change Your Life Forever* (2013)

Nancy Kline, *Time To Think: Listening to Ignite the Human Mind* (1999)

Psychology

Amy C. Edmondson, *The Fearless Organization* (2018)

Carol Dweck, *Mindset: The New Psychology of Success* (2006)

Daniel Kahneman, *Thinking Fast and Slow* (2011)

Susan Cain, *Quiet: The Power of Introverts in a World that Can't Stop Thinking* (2012)

Conclusion

About the author

I am Tahmid. I am a transformational coach who supports individuals and businesses to continually improve and be the best version of themselves. My experience stems from working in numerous public and private institutions on UK and EU policy issues.

I am passionate about Diversity and Inclusion, personal development, and organisational development. I see value in supporting the development of people that make up our workforce through empowerment and giving clearer direction. I also work to improve the processes and systems within organisations that we use on a day-to-day basis to make our jobs better and more enjoyable, with improved customer satisfaction.

I greatly believe in the importance of Diversity and Inclusion in the modern economy. I have experience working on race, having developed race training material, and presented at senior boards with recommendations on how to improve racial diversity in the workplace.

Outside of work, I love to travel and learn languages. I speak English, French and Spanish and enjoy language learning as a hobby. To wind down I also do yoga (when I get the chance!)

TAHMID
CHOWDHURY
COACH & WRITER